Awakening
in the Paradox
OF DARKNESS

GARY TZU, PhD

Copyright © 2014 by Gary Tzu

First Edition – April 2014

ISBN

978-1-4602-4051-9 (Hardcover)

978-1-4602-4052-6 (Paperback)

978-1-4602-4053-3 (eBook)

All rights reserved.

No part of this publication may be reproduced in any form, or by any means, electronic or mechanical, including photocopying, recording, or any information browsing, storage, or retrieval system, without permission in writing from the publisher.

Produced by:

FriesenPress

Suite 300 – 852 Fort Street

Victoria, BC, Canada V8W 1H8

www.friesenpress.com

Distributed to the trade by The Ingram Book Company

Contents

Introduction
Non-dual Awakening in Darkness xi

Part One
Death of the Seeker: The Luminous Night Reveals Itself 1
    1 Dissolving Ego's Dream of Specialness 3
    2 No Goal: Accepting Hopelessness and Failurehood 7
    3 No Mind, Not Even Non-dual Ideals 11
    4 The Emptiness of the Heart 16
    5 No Remedy: Accepting There is No Way Out 21

Part Two
The Grey Realm: Stuck in Limbo 25
    6 The Positive Thinking Sinkhole 27
    7 The Underbelly Narcissist: Frozen in Complaints 32
    8 Addictive Rituals to Heal Inadequacy 38
    9 Escaping Nothingness 45
    10 Losing Motivation: Running on Empty 51

Part Three

Hanging On: The Realm of the Blues 55

  11 Clinging to the Sanctuary of the Other 56

  12 Death of a Loved One:
     An Invitation to Accept Our Own Death 64

  13 Waiting for Lightning to Strike 68

Part Four

The Black Realm of Terror: Fear and Trauma 75

  14 Managing Fear Reinforces Fear 77

  15 The Mother of All Fears: The Fear of Non-existence 83

  16 Trauma: Healing through Catharsis and
     Embodied Experiencing 88

  17 The Missing Ingredients: Choiceless Awareness
     and Accepting Death 93

  18 Healing Childhood Abandonment 101

  19 The Deep Wound: A Non-dual Approach to
     Sexual Abuse Healing 105

Part Five

Veiled Darkness: Diving into the Deep Dark Realms 117

  20 Past Life Trauma: Finding the Missing Key 118

  21 Intra-uterine Trauma: The Pain of Being Born 122

  22 Hell Realm Trauma: From Enduring Terror to
     Finding the Light Within the Darkness 128

Part Six

Embracing the Bedazzling Mystery 135

  23 Ordinary and Joyously Useless: Just to Be Is Enough 137

  24 Embracing Imperfection 141

25 Relaxing into Sublime Stillness 146

26 Seeing through the Desire for Non-dual Teacherhood 150

27 Active Infinity, Passive Infinity 155

28 Never Born, Never Died: The Ultimate Medicine 160

29 Play: Enjoying the Dance and Love of Existence 163

References 169

Disclaimer

The information provided in this book is designed to provide helpful information on the subjects discussed. This book is not meant to be used, nor should it be used, to diagnose or treat any medical or psychological condition. For diagnosis or treatment of any medical or psychological problem, consult your own physician or psychologist. Neither the publisher nor the author are responsible for any specific medical or psychological health needs that may require medical or psychological supervision and are not liable for any damages or negative consequences from any treatment, action, application or preparation, to any person reading or following the information in this book. References are provided for informational purposes only and do not constitute endorsement of any texts, websites or other sources.

Other Books by Gary Tzu

—

Beyond Addiction to Awakening

To some brilliant teachers of being along the way, Osho, Papaji, and A. H. Almaas.

To Marcia for her wondrous display of love.

To Craig and Brian who keep throwing logs onto my fire of writing.

And to all my non-dual friends who said we need a book from you on awakening through the dark realms.

INTRODUCTION
Non-dual Awakening in Darkness

*The Great Way is not difficult
for those who have no preferences.
When love and hate are both absent,
everything becomes clear and undisguised.
Make the smallest distinction, however,
and heaven and earth are set infinitely apart.
If you wish to see the truth,
then hold no opinion for or against.
The struggle of what one likes and what
one dislikes is the disease of the mind.*

Sosan, Third Chinese Patriarch of Zen

When I look back at my non-dual journey, it seems ironic that, even though I started out on the quest for non-dual awakening and enlightenment desiring the *white light* goodies of love, bliss, ecstasy, serenity, and enlightenment, my actual awakening and transformation came through exploring the realms of the dark night. Through living out the nightmare of perpetually being caught in a separate self, to plunging into the dark valley of death and non-existence, to healing the pain and integrating the resulting hatred of physical abuse, to exploring past life trauma, to learning to relax into apparent *hell* while accepting no escape, and finally ultimately seeing there was nothing that could be done to create a sanctuary in existence—awakened existence revealed itself through these apparent dark realms. Darkness, once accepted, revealed a paradoxical light at its very core. It revealed life within death, full presence within ecstatic absence, and the moment spread throughout eternity. Who would have known that within the most profound darkness is contained a brilliant translucent light, a midnight black sun, the light of which reveals that no concepts are real, no thoughts are real; there exists instead a vast interconnected existence, all of which is within our own awareness.

All of our most dreaded darkness experiences are portals to the non-dual. With choiceless awareness and no-judgment, if we let go of our need to survive as separate selves, it becomes apparent that freedom is available, right here, right now. The good news then is that awakening is available right in the middle of our most apparently awful experiences. In my own journey, this non-dual relaxing into *what is* started with accepting the darkness of hopelessness and failurehood after fruitlessly seeking enlightenment. This relaxation carried on with issues such as fear, trauma, non-existence, past life memories, dark emotions, absolute nothingness, and hell realm experiences. All these experiences were embraced with the understanding of surrender, no-judgment, and letting go of attachment to individual separate self existence. With this, the beautiful translucent non-dual reality revealed itself right within these realms themselves.

Thus it became obvious that what is called for is to reverse our usual strategy of dealing with the dark realms of existence. This book is meant as a clarion call, inviting readers to work through the dark realms and heal themselves into awakening. We could even call these realms dark holes, places where inwardly we have lost touch with our essence, our consciousness, our divine nature. We perceive these dark holes both without and within. We have tried running away from them, repressing them, denying them, coping with them, picking ourselves up by our bootstraps against them, but it all has not worked. Seeing the hopelessness of avoidance, we can take the plunge, become one with our dark realms, and heal from within through non-dual awareness.

Shades of Darkness

In this book, we will look at a spectrum of dark realm experiences that range from the banal grey of ashes, frozenness and limbo states, to the blue realms of anguished love and long unrepentant suffering, to the black hole deathly realms such as the terror of fear, annihilation, non-existence and trauma, to the eternal depths of blackness in which fates worse than death must be worked through. It is important to understand that these experiences and shades of the dark realms intermingle. While each of us may have a particular dark hole to deal with, in many ways each of us is destined to deal with the whole array of dark realms in one way or another. So, this book becomes an invitation for a full spectrum embracement of non-dual being in which we willingly allow ourselves to be transformed by the multiple aspects of the dark realms of existence.

Choiceless Awareness and No Judgment

Throughout this book, as we are invited to dive into disowned aspects of being—at one level so unique, but at a deeper level so similar—we will constantly be embracing the theme of choiceless awareness.[1] As Sosan says, the struggle of what one likes and what one dislikes is the disease of the mind. We are invited to sit in our wounds—those places we have avoided—with choiceless awareness and no judgment, so that true healing can take place. By dropping our split-mind, our judgments, our commentaries, and our stories and just sitting in *what is*, the consciousness of existence—our awareness—can flow through and expand into our holes, and the energy becomes very spacious and re-connected to being. We will be returning to the process of embracing choiceless awareness many times in this book to help the reader get a deeper understanding of this process. Healing occurs through learning to *be one with what is*. In choiceless awareness, dark holes internally thaw and re-fill with the essence of existence. Dark emotions such as fear, sadness, and abandonment can be befriended and then lovingly expand like a celebratory heartfelt aloneness. Even long-dreaded experiences such as the fear of non-existence and so-called *hell* are unpacked as we feel the light of awareness even in the experience of absolute darkness.

In the journey to non-dual awakening, to come home and feel the vast splendour of existence, we recognize that so many of us have been sidetracked by managing these holes in one way or another. In this hijacked state, we do not fully enjoy our existence. As non-dual teacher A. H. Almaas pointed out, we will do almost anything except actually heal these holes.[2] This book is about learning to heal the holes directly, to allow them to be transformational opportunities for awakening. What good is our non-dual awakening if we can not resolutely use our non-dual insights and understanding to deal with these most difficult human experiences and find an even deeper non-dual awakening in these experiences themselves. So, in this book, we are going right to the experiences that we are resistant to face. Standing like an ostrich, with your head in the sand, ignoring these holes does not work, nor does running away from them like a frightened rabbit. The healing and awakening is right inside the experience itself.

The Healing Paradox

Come along and share the ride. I trust that you can embrace the transformational journey offered through some of the most dreaded human experiences, for it points to non-dual awakening that is implicit in the experience itself. It may appear, at times, that we delve deeply into the past, but all healing is actually in the present moment. In fact, whether we are talking about the past, present or future, as we move beyond the limitations of our minds, we see that all of eternity is contained within the moment. This is where freedom lies: in the holistic celebration of interconnected oneness that is the here and now. To affect healing, it may appear that we move across time, when, in fact, all healing is in this moment in which all of existence is contained.

Thus, before we start our exploration of the journey of healing and awakening into non-dual realization, it is important to acknowledge the inherent paradox. The process is not a journey from one place to another: it is really a journey from here to here, and thus all healing into the radiant interconnected energy of existence is available in this moment.

PART ONE

Death of the Seeker: The Luminous Night Reveals Itself

It is paradoxical, the journey into non-dual awakening, in that all of self is taken away so that existence can reveal itself. All that is required is the ongoing art of dying in which nothing is accumulated at all. We can't accumulate anything whatsoever. What is called for is a state of poverty, inner spiritual poverty. Almaas described this state as leaving us with nothing to hang onto so that this surrender allows the dark emptiness to fully reveal itself:

> Accepting our total poverty and not asking for more allows us to surrender whatever is left of our selfhood. This surrender reveals that the emptiness of poverty is simply the inscrutable darkness of the Divine Essence, which is obscured as lack because of subtle veils. Now, however, the emptiness of poverty reveals itself as the majestic and luminous darkness of the mystery of being. The dark emptiness becomes a luminous night, the mystical midnight sun, the very essence of divinity, the divine darkness that is the source of all light.[1]

In this part of the book, we will look at inner veils, aspects of the inner self that need to be let go of in the non-dual journey so that the dark night can reveal itself. Our ego and accompanying specialness has to go; our striving, our sense of finding the answer, our sense of being a separate individual, all our knowledge and concepts that we hang onto in our minds, our sense of being a loving and good person, and even our sense of finding and having the answer all have to be surrendered to the dark night. When we are inwardly naked and transparent, when we are vulnerable and open and not hanging onto anything, the paradox of darkness reveals itself.

CHAPTER 1
Dissolving Ego's Dream of Specialness

Looking back, I can see that all of my desires for awakening lead me somewhere else, to some future moment in time. In this way, I was going to have a tense mind forever because I still had this huge goal of idealized enlightenment, some magical awakening in the future. A mind with a goal is always stressed because it cannot relax in this moment. It is always trying to get somewhere. The nature of desiring and goal-setting is that nothing is okay in the present moment. It is always a rejection of the present moment as one is saying that this moment is not good enough, but one hopes that, in a future moment, everything will be attained and be okay. My trying had not worked at all. Trying itself is suffering. I saw that I had been caught seeking, chasing my perpetual desire for awakening. It always points to the future, and it is never in this moment. I had to stop and take the risk of finding out what was actually in the moment. I could see that I needed to give up the chase and stop striving so desperately after a goal I would never reach. I needed to let go of the anguish of unfulfilled effort before I lost myself down a bottomless pit of eternal becoming—and never being.

Exhaustion brought me to my knees. I realized there was actually no place to get to. I could give up pursuing awakening because it had been an idle dream, a dream for the future. I could give it up for what was real, which is to say *the actual moment*. And as I became attuned to the moment, a shocking revelation hit, I could see awakening and enlightenment were actually just concepts; they did not exist in the moment. I also could see something else that was totally shocking.

I was not special at all.

Nothingness: Dissolving Ego's Dream of Specialness

I was not special; I was just a narcissist and entirely ordinary. I was not the answer, I was the problem. My whole spiritual journey had just been one long trip to reaffirm my narcissism, the specialness of who I was. So, in exhaustion and nothingness, I confronted my own narcissism.

A. H. Almaas observed, early on in life, that in grappling with a lack of mirroring and needing to survive, we escape into narcissistic strategies to establish our specialness.[1] As I looked back at my whole life, I could see the extent to which I had propped up my ego with goals, motivations, future aspirations, and even spiritual pursuits. I realized I had carried within myself an infantile dream of specialness from a very young age. It is like God plays a joke on us all. As we are born, he says, "You're special..." *to each and every one of us*. And I bit that—hook, line, and sinker.

I was special, and I was on this ultimate trip in life to prove how special I was. Unaware, I set myself up for misery. I graduated from high school, went to university, and within two years was in law school. My fervent specialness had hit an all-time high. A few of years later, when my enthusiasm for a law career crashed at the start of actual practice, I dove into Eastern contemplation and awakening traditions with the same over-the-top zest that had initially marked my law career. I had totally changed life paths but was still carrying on, grasping at my own fundamental specialness.

Enlightenment became my new goal, and so I approached it as I did all my goals back then, which is to say aggressively. I tried to storm the gates of awakening, convinced that such a lofty goal required heroic effort, and so heroic effort is what I gave.

As could be predicted, things did not work out at all. Darkness eventually came over my seeking. I had started out with an abundance of bliss and ecstasy emanating from a stringent daily structure of regular three-hour meditations. But, over time, all this began to fade. It was not an overnight transition, but gradually all of the exciting experiences of bliss, cosmic consciousness experiences, ecstasy and serenity started to lose their shine. I began to recognize all of these experiences were just temporary, and nothing really stuck. And in my desperation I ended up trying just about everything. Talk therapy, encounter therapy, bioenergetics, primal screaming, vippasanā meditation, darkness mediation, long distance running, humming mediation, hollow bamboo mediation, self-inquiry, self-remembrance, letting go, surrendering, doing nothing—it all worked for a while and then faded. None of those promising blossoms ever bore fruit. What had started out with so much ecstatic promise, turned ugly and depressing. I had started out looking for bliss, ecstasy and love, and now all I really had was pain, disillusionment, and misery. I had been brought to my knees, not by prayer, but by exhaustion and desperation.

The Master of the Universe Falls into Being and Nothingness

So, the realization had come. I had been living the life of a common narcissist. What was shocking to me was to recognize that my entire search for awakening was nothing more than an attempted affirmation of my own *specialness*, a fundamental narcissism dressed up in spiritual clothing. Actually it made me laugh, for I had fallen into what Patrick Carnes called the "Master of the Universe" pattern characteristic of narcissistic addicts in which all is justified because of a person's belief in their own "uniqueness, specialness, or superiority" and their assertion that they are made of "the right stuff."[2] Now, I could feel myself really falling into the abyss that I had danced around for years. It actually made me laugh. It became apparent that my desire for awakening and my goal of enlightenment wasn't special at all; it was very ordinary and entirely narcissistic, and millions of others had the same goal. I actually had nothing in my sights but a narcissistic dream of the ego.

Seeing the fakeness of my so-called specialness, I could feel the ground give way beneath my feet. It had been all narcissism. The apparent "master of the universe" fell into the ocean of nothingness. I saw the fakeness of my need to be mirrored in a special way. I fell out of my head into my belly and found myself in the chasm of the present moment, the original simple abiding presence. Rather than reconstituting my gig of narcissism and being swept away in ego activity, I now had the chance to be vulnerably attuned to the great chasm of being, to be one with the nothingness.

CHAPTER 2
No Goal: Accepting Hopelessness and Failurehood

Out of discovering my fundamental narcissism, I came to realize that I am the problem. It was so clear. Anything I did would just create more problems. Whatever I did would only feed the problem, for I would be bolstering my ego in the moment.

All my hopes were simply false. Hopes always involve the future. I had always been dreaming about the future. For many years, no matter how tired I became questing for awakening, somehow I managed to be hopeful for the future. It was shocking that I had descended into the abyss years earlier—in a world collapse at the end of law school—but still managed to hang onto the lifejacket of hope for many years through my desire for awakening. I could now see that all of this hoping was a false strategy of the ego, an addiction of the ego to keep it alive. Now in the moment, there was no hope and no ego. Letting go of hope just happened all by itself through seeing it as a false strategy of ego. Hope was truly hopeless, even hanging onto hopelessness was hopeless, so hope was seen as an addiction, and it dropped by itself.

My *self* had been unsuccessful in its attempt to move beyond its own perceived boundaries; it had been a total failure. When I understood and accepted my own *failurehood*, my efforts ceased. In my exhaustion, both hope and impulse dropped into an ocean of nothingness. What I had perceived as self was extinguished, subsumed in the vast blackness of eternity and came to rest in non-existence devoid of judgement. There was an acceptance that resting in this black sky of non-existence could go on forever, and there was acceptance in this apparent being. I had seen the futility of effort and rested in the understanding that nothing could be done—there was truly no place to go. That phrase—*nothing could be done*—I'd heard it a thousand times before, but now I understood its full impact. All had been done. Hanging on was futile. I was letting go through being utterly open to existence.

Accepting Being Lost in the Dark Night: Existence Reveals Itself

When your material and spiritual words collapse upon themselves and you accept your own hopelessness and failurehood, there is no longer any ground into which the narcissist ego can take root, and you are left adrift in the eternal moment. I had been here before but always with a subtle judgment related to being "lost in eternity", and was never able to just relax into it. Now, there was a recognition that "being lost" was exactly where I needed to be.

Finally, I accepted this vast dark night of existence and made no effort to save or resurrect myself. There was something serene in this acceptance. It felt like I was beyond any existence, beyond any being, beyond a self or other—an utterly peaceful black night of absence and non-existence.

This serene relaxation stretched over the course of a week and culminated on a Saturday afternoon looking out my window while resting in an easy chair. Effort, manipulation, my hanging on, my dreams of awakening—they had all dissolved into the black ocean of emptiness, and with that there was an acceptance of death. Resting in this depth, suddenly, out of the blackness, the brilliant light of existence emerged, vast and translucence. I laughed in amazement as the hidden splendour of existence revealed itself, as out of this mysterious darkness came this brilliant light. It was shocking, out of the darkest night, came a wondrous bedazzling light. I was amazed. The light was everywhere. It was as if all of existence were enlightened. I looked out the window and saw the sun coming across the coulees and was aware that the whole of existence was dancing and alive with energy. There was nobody present to receive awakening, but awakening was here, everything intensely beautiful in the moment, everything celebratory and alive with energy. Even my own body was on fire, but there was no sense of a separate body being there.

No Goal: The Wisdom of Non-Attainment

The illumination of existence was shocking to this being. It came as a gift from existence through simply accepting how profoundly lost I was and that there was nowhere to get to, no goal. The acceptance of being lost in eternity was the gateway to the opening up of existence.

I became aware that my desire for awakening had been an obstacle. I could see that, with no goal, nowhere to get to, the moment was enough. All along, I already was where I was headed. It only became available to my awareness when I gave up. I did not need to seek it—existence was already there. I just needed to get out of the way. Seeing through the goal of awakening allowed existence to reveal itself. No effort was needed, but apparently I had to go through a lot of effort to relax into effortlessness. As long as I had still been hoping for spiritual success, there was a implicit dyad of Me plus existence—two discrete elements—which was one too many.

Nobody becomes awakened. The one trying to be awakened is the problem. This is the egoic narcissist. As long as there is a goal of awakening, there is the consciousness of a separate being. When the goal of awakening is relaxed and let go—in utter failurehood and perfect hopelessness—the separate self dissolves, and existence reveals itself. Nothing is actually attained, what is already here reveals itself. There is a grand cosmic humour to all of this, as it is seen that awakening has been present all the way along, all of existence is already enlightened. We just get so swept away with the desire for awakening that we cannot see it in the moment.

CHAPTER 3
No Mind, Not Even Non-dual Ideals

Looking closely, one sees that mind is always dependent upon what was in the past. Nothing from mind is ever new. Mind is always based upon repetition, memory, relying on the known and accumulations from the past. Mind cannot meet the freshness of the new, of this moment, as it is filled with the thoughts and apparent knowledge it has accumulated from the past. In doing so, the new is dusted with the ashes of the past and is not perceived in its fresh state.

A realization arises that the whole mind itself is the disease. Wanting to intellectually construct and reconstruct the journey in our little minds and grab onto the secrets of existence, utterly fails to help us embrace what is beyond the known. As J. Krishnamurti spent a lifetime lecturing, freedom is beyond the known.[1] The key is, rather than constantly judging existence with mind, we need to embrace what is, in order to be one with existence through choiceless awareness.

However, going beyond mind can be tricky because the mind believes in its ability to help. For example, when there has been an awakening experience, the mind wants to hold awakening firmly in its grasp, to erect a sanctuary around some mind-invented secrets of awakening to forever perpetuate the experience. Unfortunately, there is no method for the mind to go beyond itself, and thus one can soon be back to spinning and grabbing in an attempt to hang onto one remedy or another, to secure awakening, not realizing that the grasping and grabbing nature of mind is itself the problem. One needs to see that the only answer to awakening is to embrace an ongoing total demolition of the mind. It must become clear to the seeker that thinking cannot do the job. How can any methods of the known embrace the mystery of the unknown? So, instead of believing that our minds can continue to deliver us, we need to become aware of the limitations of mind and be ever watchful; no concept, technique, or semblance of knowledge can be our salvation. For the mind provides no answer. We have to let go of our addictive pattern of always turning to the mind for something to grab onto. There is no answer for the mind.

When the mind's knowledge, techniques, secret motivations, or goals are dropped, what remains is what was expressed in Bodhidharma's famous reply to the question "Who are you?" posed by the Chinese emperor in 500 A.D.: "No knowing."[2] Everything had been dropped, and Bodhidharma is responding from simple, pure innocence and standing in no knowing. Being present, in each moment, in the consciousness of "no knowing" is utter divine innocence, and what emerges is the awareness of the vast interconnected consciousness energy of existence.

The Small Brain: Wrapped Up in Non-dual Ideals

The difficulty with the mind is that it can actually be the great pretender. Embracing awakening from the consciousness of the mind propels one to read many non-dual books, listen to discourses from non-dual teachers, experiment with meditation and self-inquiry techniques and focus primarily on an intellectual approach. This can amount to playing at the awakening game with zest, a great head game of non-dual concepts and clichés. The trouble is that a person can be so well read that he or she can spin out the non-dual clichés pretty convincingly, but it is obvious from a perspective of beingness that there has been no fundamental awakening, or what Adyashanti has called a "change in occupancy" from the separate self to resting in existence itself.[3]

A subtler version of the problem is that a person may have awakened into non-dual being and can abide fairly consistently in this consciousness but still be hanging onto the mind or small brain in subtle ways. For a time, this was my problem. I was residing in my belly of awareness, but I was going back into my head to try to figure out how to be helpful to bring non-dual awareness to others, very counter-productive. I was caught in the non-dual ideal of The Bodhisattva Vow to bring other people to awakening. One day, I realized this was just madness, mind coming in through the back door, and misery incorporated. I let this attachment to being helpful go.

By just being natural, spontaneous, in the moment, and not planning beyond this moment, the process of helping others started taking off in its own way. It was all just a happening. It was like my brain was always saying *strategize, you have to be driving the car*, and then one day, I realized the vehicle was going down the road by itself, and I could just relax in the passenger side, for everything was happening by itself. It made me laugh. Seeing the pattern, it all could be just dropped. I was free to enjoy the play of existence.

Just abiding in nothingness—the empty sky of existence—without the mind's interference meant that I could spontaneously let nothingness have free reign. In this nothingness, one sees that there is nothing to grab onto. One just rests in nothingness in each moment, with no inner voice or psychological functioning. One is in cessation, where functioning happens as ego and so-called *personal will* has been dropped. One just has peaceful functioning in the moment. When something arises in the moment, it is just watched but not grabbed onto or repelled from. Along with this, there is no attaching onto the "I" thought, the lynchpin that holds the mirage of the separate self together.

Now we will turn to a small case example. Throughout the book, I will be using cases from my non-dual therapy practice in which I work with people in groups and individually. Here, we have an example from one of my abiding in non-dual being groups.

The Limitation of Awakening Only Through Mind

Frequently, people have awakenings primarily limited to mind. Jim, a non-dual philosopher, was like that. He had awakened through focusing on "I am." And now as a guest in my group he looked over at me and said to me:

"I don't get what you mean, relax into being."

"Exactly," I said. "You are still in your head."

This can be a tricky issue. A person can have had an experience of awakening in the mind, felt the transcendent oneness, and even a sense of "I am" that connects with all of existence. Yet the problem with being identified through the head—the mind—is that it is still a fixed position, and there can be a kind of superior nonchalance with it, the narcissism of the non-dual mind. A person has not yet seen that they are still using mind to get to the answer, and in his or her own way, there has not been a whole breakdown of the mind into being. When one grabs onto transcendence and vast interconnection, there can be a subtle attachment that forms a sense of superiority in the person. Even this has to be let go of.

Out of the head, through the heart and into the belly is where the energy needs to go. Adyashanti laid out how awakening is through the mind, heart and belly, and all three aspects need to be fully awakened.[4] The problem with just a mind awakening is that there is not a total relaxation into the intimacy of what is. There is a lack of total vulnerability and engagement with what is. Total vulnerability means embracing the wisdom of insecurity. It is total vulnerability in each moment with no knowledge to hang onto. Nobody is superior as we all are swept away in the vulnerable interconnected vastness where we embrace a certain no-mindedness and a blown-wide-open loving heart and do not hang onto our separate selves in our guts. We will now turn to where so many get caught, trying to be a loving and good person in the heart.

CHAPTER 4
The Emptiness of the Heart

One day, while I was working in a non-dual individual psychotherapy session with a community social worker, Sonja, she told me that it was very important for her to be seen as a loving person. I laughed.

"Can you see the narcissism behind that?" I asked. "You want the world to mirror back to you how special you are with your loving ways. Can you see that it is a managed thing? I suppose you also want to be seen as a good person as well."

She laughed as well. "Yes of course."

I said to her, "Being seen as a loving and good person is just narcissism. You want your loving and goodness to be mirrored back to you so you can keep up your identity as a special person. That is just ego. You're being trapped into self-representations of love and goodness. It is a con."

Sonja stared back at me, shocked. I continued. "You need to let go of all those spiritual identity games to feel special. See how ordinary your desire to be special is. I bet you know somebody who thinks he or she is a good person, but you can see how this person manipulates people, is inauthentic, and in many ways not very loving at all."

She smiled in agreement. These are what the Jungians call *shadow issues*.[1] Our ego is trying to present itself in a certain pleasing way, a *persona* which is the Greek word for mask. Behind the mask, there are all these shadow issues of what really is going on.

People on the quest for spirituality and awakening often spend so much time trying to imitate spiritual ideals like loving-kindness and compassion. This is just the old game of ego self-improvement, dressed up. I have a counsellor friend, Ken, who can be quite nonchalant and arrogant with his so-called *spiritual wisdom* who actually does loving-kindness meditations on a regular basis while at the same time carrying on with his arrogant ways. He can not see the contradiction.

How can this contradiction be resolved? Through awareness, one has to see the built-in failure of striving for these egoic ideals and see all of the ego's demand for spiritual specialness as simple narcissism. Face the fire of the ego con of trying to be a loving person and recognize it for narcissism, dressed up in spiritual clothing. The way out is to see, in this demand to be special, that you are the not the solution, but the problem. Face the death of all of this loving-goodness nonsense and let it all go, with no identity or story attached. Take the risk of authentically coming from your own nature.

In my experience, when a person can see that this demand for specialness through needing to be a loving and good person is just ego and in fact the problem, the person can in fact laugh and let it all go. Seeing that it has been a complete con allows you to rest in your own nature and be a natural person. And here is the magical thing: Just resting in being, a person discovers the vast interconnectedness of existence, oneness with the mountains, trees, stars, animals and human beings. This connectedness *makes* you a loving person, not by effort, but by feeling the loving interconnected presence. It is not a put on, it is just a matter of feeling connected with all beings.

Related to this con of trying to be a good and loving person is the façade of being a deeply emotional person. In this one, a person claims to be so feelings oriented and sensitive to what is going on that they find it overwhelming, and this justifies emotionally reactive behaviour. As Adyashanti said, this person needs to find out how much separate self ego is arising all of the time in the middle of these emotions.[2]

A good example is to examine to the experience of being hurt. Osho used to joke that the story of the universe is "You, me, hurt." We are constantly talking about how we got hurt by what somebody said to us. The fact of the matter is that the other person does not actually hurt us, we do it to ourselves. In the moment that the person says the so-called hurtful comment to you, just as you are about to react, see if there is actually any separate being inside. The insult will come, and if it not grabbed by an apparent ego, it just comes and falls away. But instead our apparent ego gets in there and says, "How dare he make fun of me." Look closely, the assumed ego, the separate voice "I" has grabbed the feeling and run with it. But if we look closely at this so-called "I", we do not see a substantial separate identity person there, just a thought of "I" that is treated as if it is an identity. When we look closely at this thought of an apparent "I", it dissolves back to stillness all by itself. So really insults are received not by an "I" but by a nobody. And nobody needs to grab onto them, the insults can slide away like water off a duck's back.

In a university class that I was teaching a few years ago, a student actually asked me in front of the whole class, "Where did you get your PhD, from a Crackerjack box? Are you just making up the course material as you go along?"

I laughed out loud. The insult was funny, it arose and fall away, and no separate "I" was needed to be grabbed on to.

The trick then is to look at our emotions, and see how much of it is perpetuated by our ego's sense of separate self-identity. The illusionary "I" grabs the feeling and runs with it. And as Byron Katie explains, it is from here that the first thought of "I" lands and more stories are born and take off.[3] With awareness, we can just let the emotions arise and fall away and do nothing to manage them. This perspective doesn't deny feelings like the sadness you feel when you hear that a long time friend has passed away or the early morning feeling of joy of a sparkling coulee run along a river trail. All of this can be felt, the trick is not let an apparent "I" get in there and start either being attracted to certain feelings, or trying to repel certain other feelings. Let the feelings be met with awareness, and see them arise and fall away.

The Empty Heart

As we take the ego out of our emotions, we can experience ourselves being so much more intimate with life as feelings can be felt in a raw way in the moment and then fall away with no interference from an apparent somebody. So, on the one hand, we can be more intimate and spontaneous with what is happening, yet on the other hand we can be more relaxed as we abide in non-dual being and are not constantly managing our feelings.

When a close relative or friend dies, we see the usual psychodrama play with the funeral and the proceedings of so many people getting caught up in the story of this shouldn't have happened. The ego is getting in there with its complaint, "It should not have happened." But actually the person died, it happened. As Byron Katie would say, people are constantly creating misery for themselves by arguing with reality. The person died, it is sad, that is okay. With a vast spacious loving empty heart, the sadness arises and falls away back into a vast loving presence. All is accepted.

In fact, this vast empty heart, in which no feeling or story or demand is tightly hung on to, allows the magical presence of the guest, the absolute heart of existence, to show up. The emptiness of the heart allows the absolute heartfeltness and love of existence to be experienced. As expressed in this following poem by Almaas, all mind aspects must be melted away in the heart for the guest to arrive:

Annihilate mind in heart,
Divorce heart from all relationships,
And then love,
Love passionately,
Consume yourself with passion
for the secret one.
When you are absolutely poor,
When you are no more,
Then the Guest will appear [4]

CHAPTER 5
No Remedy: Accepting There is No Way Out

In my own journey, at a certain point, I realized there was no answer for my seeking. There was no remedy and no way out. There was no sanctuary for my mind to hang onto. In my exhaustion, with the dizzying madness prospect that grasping at some remedy or escape or secret could go on forever, a "fuck it" came out of the depths of my being, and I relaxed.

A funny thing happened, as I relaxed and enjoyed the moment, divine existence showed up in all of its intensity. Of course, it had been here all along, I had just been too busy seeking, to be able to see it. I was seeking with my eyes closed! The search took me on a wild goose chase only to eventually deliver me back to the moment. It was so simple, "This is it." I laughed at the ridiculousness of the whole seeking game. It is all so clear, right here, right now. Perfection.

Desperate Madness: Clients on the Edge

I knew it might be helpful to share this end of seeking awareness with the non-dual therapy clients I worked with. It was complicated though because it seemed necessary for the apparent person to become like an overly ripe fruit before the illusion of self can be seen through. In my own journey, the intensity to work it all out was very much over the top. It was like it was reaching a boiling point. I was just desperate to find the answer and round and round my mind went trying to figure out the keys to the mystery of existence. I knew that I was getting close to madness when I started to feel that this could go on forever. Then, out of the blue, came the answer, almost like a present from existence: "There is no answer." Immediate relief came; it was like I was trying to get out of the prison and, when I realized there was no way out, I could relax. And the paradox was, as I relaxed and enjoyed the what is, the prison dissolved all by itself.

 I have tried to reach clients through writing about "the end of the line" experience in which a person seems to be at a desperate "suicide or surrender" phase. Clients from around the world have contacted me in this desperate madness phase with a sense of perhaps needing to commit suicide, as existence now appears doomed. I, too, in the middle of my end of the line madness time, had fleeting thoughts of suicide. These thoughts did not last long, though, as I had always accepted the sense that we keep reincarnating until we become free, and this would only then make matters worse for me if I killed myself. I would have a whole new level of problems to deal with. Surrender was my only option.

 End of the line seekers often contact me for help because they know something very wrong has happened. They are trapped in their seeking, trapped in their minds. Even though they have seen every non-dual teacher under the sun and have begun to think their existence is doomed, they still want to do more seeking. Even though they are becoming very desperate, something deep inside is saying that they have not tried hard enough. It is like they have been totally hypnotized by the Protestant Work Ethic, requiring more work and effort regardless of exhaustion.

It is here, in the middle of this mad vortex of seeking, that I work with people to see that there is no way out, there is no answer for their separate self existence. If this realization is seen and accepted, it can bring a feeling of total sublime serenity. It is like there is breakdown of the seeking mind into stillness. It brings humour later when one looks around seeing the insanity of those so desperately trying to work it out, as if their little brain could catch within its grasp all of the secrets of existence. Giving up is one thing that the mind does not like to do. But giving up is exactly what is called for.

Kelly's Return to Absolute Hopelessness

What I have noticed is that people can get tragically caught up in intricate systems of awakening that go on and on. Zen, Tibetan Buddhism, Sufism, Adi Da, Osho, there are lots of intricate pathways, layers and layers, so the seeking goes on and on. Some individuals have been at it for twenty, thirty, forty years and yet still can't see the big picture. In relation to this predicament, Krishnamurti pointed to the "first and last freedom."[1] Freedom has to be the first step. "Letting go" has to be the first step, not the last. And if much seeking has happened, it all has to be let go of, so letting go is reclaimed as the first step.

And what is funny is that often people will have a huge transformational awakening experience and then go back and put the chains back on. For example, Kelly, a woman in her fifties, had been involved with various spiritual teachers in the Tibetan Buddhist tradition. In her mid-twenties, while being involved with the teachings of Chogyam Trungpa, she had a profound experience of accepting the absolute hopelessness of seeking, and existence opened up to her in serene stillness, and everything was revealed in the moment. It is an experience that stayed with her for months. But then, later, she got re-involved in formal Tibetan Buddhist meditation teachings and was off to meditation retreats and working on "purity" and other concepts. And now, here she was talking to me thirty years later, again approaching total hopelessness after she had been seduced back to multi-levels of practice, rituals, and meditations. Her experience was almost mind-boggling. There was always something more that Kelly felt she could do, some more mediation, some more rituals, some more reading, some more listening to instructions, and on and on it went. And yet, here she was, once again feeling very exhausted, no longer being able to muster up the energy for all of these practices or the hope for another retreat.

I knew Kelly was right where she needed to be. In my work with her, I just mirrored back to her that nothing could be done and that there was no where to get to and no amount of effort could change that, and that feeling absolutely hopeless was perfect for her. She felt relieved and started to de-hypnotize the spell of hypnosis she was under that always called for more effort and more meditation. As she let this hopelessness and failurehood of effort into her consciousness, a vivid memory of her absolute hopelessness experience thirty years previous spontaneously arose. But back then, it had not totally impacted her. She had picked up the chain of effort again and drifted back into a myriad of practices and rituals. This time it was different. This time, her experience of absolute hopelessness was perfect. She could see that there was no point in picking up any of these practices again. She needed to do nothing. There was no answer, no remedy, just this.

PART TWO
The Grey Realm: Stuck in Limbo

The non-dual journey is a letting go process in which the totality of the self is surrendered. This can be very frightening to our ego and sense of being a separate person. One of the ways we have been conditioned, since early on in our lives, to make life manageable is to make deals to handle life. We want to be safe and secure, so we fixated on people, places, rituals—anything to give us a sense of solidness and security. So, rather than surrender to the vast absolute energy of existence, we tame the wildness with safe little deals that we make within ourselves and with the others around us. This is the grey realm.

We will see in this grey realm section, some of the deals we make within our lives to create a life that is more easy to cope with. We try to contain our life by focusing only on positive experiences and positive thoughts—or in some cases, we get lost in a sense of being a loser or a victim. We can feel inadequate and grey inside, and we have our little addictive rituals to overcome our insufficiency. We encounter the vast abyss of nothingness opening up within our being and run like hell to some safe compound only to lose the vastness. And finally, one day our whole motivation, our whole game, falls away, and we are left running on empty, scurrying around to find new meaning. All of these grey realm issues are just invitations to plunge into all of life and embrace existence head on rather than hiding out. Each one of these grey zone issues is a transformational portal to non-dual awakening.

CHAPTER 6
The Positive Thinking Sinkhole

So much human suffering flows from our relentless pursuit and affirmation of what we consider positive and our dogged rejection of that which we dub negative. We like the apparent positive, and dislike the apparent negative. Through our mind, we are trying to chase happiness. The problem with this mind perspective is that it involves not accepting life as it is in all its colours, and this sets us up for suffering. We are trying to make life conform to our thoughts, feelings, and expectations. Actual awakening happens through accepting life as it is.

About five years ago my older brother, who is a lawyer specializing in First Nations aboriginal law, came and spent a few days with me as he was on a quest for wholeness and feeling an attunement with non-dual being. He asked me at a coffee shop to just give him one invitation to work on. I smiled to myself and said to him:

"Stop lecturing everybody all the time about how they need to be positive. It is a complete rejection of half of life, the apparent negative."

He sat there stunned, but then said, "I will do that."

Years later he thanked me for that invitation.

It seems strange to people for me to say, "Stop trying to be so positive." What could be wrong with trying to be positive? I will cut to the chase. The problem with the positive thinking perspective is that a person is continually judging life with a discriminating mind: *This is positive, good… oh no, this is negative, that is bad, I have to overcome this. I need to be positive.*

So the person is constantly trying to fight towards the positive and control the negative, with a whole lot of judgments. It is a constant war and requires ongoing effort to try and be positive in thinking, and the negative keeps showing up. That is the complimentary aspect of life: try to be loving, non-loving shows up; try to be non-angry, anger shows up. They go together. It is like trying to have life without death or light without darkness.

The problem is that, in the whole effort to be only positive, negative aspects of life are denied, repressed, glossed over, and they morph into what the Jungian psychologists call the shadow.[1] The ego dystonic aspects, which we are trying to overcome, move into our unconsciousness as we are trying so hard to be positive that we deny and repress the apparent negative. The trouble is that apparent negative aspects are simply a part of life, and keep showing up. They are not contradictory. They are complimentary.

Fighting Hopelessness and Helplessness

Let me give you an example from Karl, a social worker friend of mine. He was reading my first book *Beyond Addiction to Awakening* and he wrote to me and said:

> The problem I have is not being comfortable in my own skin. My problem at this point in life is not being able to live in a state of calm and confident serenity. I am unable to achieve my desired goal, which is total peace of mind and total joy. AA speaks a lot about peace of mind/serenity. I want this, but I

fear I won't get it until I am at the point of total and utter despair. I hope there is pathway to 100% surrender that does not involve resignation and helplessness and hopelessness and the existential despair born of lost hope and born of the realization that one has been fooling oneself due to unrealistic optimism.

When I read this, I knew that resignation, hopelessness and helplessness was exactly what he needed to experience—as this was already in his being—but he was running away from these dark emotions. He needed to accept the hopelessness and helplessness of his whole addiction recovery project and to surrender to what is. I invited him to have a telephone consultation with me which he gratefully accepted.

In our session together he told me how much he liked the quote from J. Krishnamurti, explaining that the secret to his own state of mind and being was "I don't mind what happens". I saw this as my golden opportunity. I explained to him that this was Krishnamurti's invitation to choiceless awareness. I explained to Karl:

"In each moment, drop the mind's tendency to always be choosing and saying 'I don't like this, I like that.' A simple way of looking at this is to just embrace no-judgment. No judging in each moment."

Karl rolled with this right away as it reminded him of Jesus' saying "Judge not." So my final invitation for the day was "No judgment, just embrace what is." We wound up our telephone session with that, and Karl agreed to follow up with me in a couple of weeks.

Karl did in fact follow up a couple of weeks later. He reported that the interim time had been very turbulent. A grievance had been filed against him at work, and he had to meet with a superior to determine if disciplinary measures would be enacted against him. Karl reported:

We were all close enough to see the colour of each other's eyes. I looked directly into the boss's eyes, and he returned the gaze. It was a fairly intimate encounter, but I noticed how comfortable I felt. Surely, I am not the only one to have the experience of sitting in the "hot seat" in the boss's office. I imagine it would typically be experienced as exceptionally uncomfortable for the typical professional to be sitting in that chair. For some of my peers, it may have even felt like an electric chair. But for me, it was comfortable. I was with the union rep, and the three of us sat there for forty-five minutes. On occasion, I heard myself speaking words, which came out softly and sincerely. I noticed a sense of ease in my voice and the best way to describe the experience of speaking was that it felt natural/authentic. On the inside, it felt quiet, still and peaceful.

What had happened for Karl? He told me:
"You said that is the quality of being where one lives and breathes and has their being in non-judging. That was your advice to me. I suppose some part of me took your advice to heart and acted on it."

Karl was in the flow, staying in no-judgment—"at rest in the silent witness" is the way he described it.

This new way of being, Karl noticed, had infused his whole life. A new romantic relationship suddenly opened up, after an unexpected divorce the previous year. He felt relaxed and authentic, and now he only prayed if it came over him spontaneously, and he kept mindful of not beating himself up. He reported feeling tremendous gratitude.

"Gary," he said, "this is a new level of consciousness."

All of this came out of Karl going beyond his positive thinking preoccupation, embracing no judgment and accepting what is. He had a situation of a grievance against him that could have been seen as terrible, and normally he would have been all worked up about it, but instead he just embraced no judgment, and authentically embraced "what was" in the moment. As a result, he felt natural, authentic and in the flow. He was ready to accept any outcome, but later found out the complaint had been dismissed.

When we try to be positive, it is like we are trying to live in only one half of life, even though every concept implies its opposite. Happiness implies sadness, and if we have only room for happiness in our life what do we do with sadness when it comes up? Instead of fighting the so-called negative, if we embrace no judgment we soon find it is hard to keep track of what is positive and what is negative and everything intermingles in a grand acceptance of life. I always liked the saying of Sosan, the third Chinese Patriarch Zen Master. He wrote in his *Hsin Hsin Ming: The Book of Nothing* over a thousand years ago:

"If you wish to see the truth then hold no opinion for or against. The struggle of what one likes and what one dislikes is the disease of the mind."[2]

We see that it is the discriminatory mind with all of its preferences, choices and judgments that keeps us in emotional hell—keeps us suffering. If we can actually see it, we don't even have to use no judgment as a technique, for seeing the misery and suffering of our judging mind stops it, at which point we can embrace no judgment and choiceless awareness, and existence reveals itself.

CHAPTER 7
The Underbelly Narcissist: Frozen in Complaints

Zen Master Hakuin wrote in his "Song of Meditation" there is no difference between awakened beings and others except the frozen state of others:

> All beings are from the very beginning Buddhas.
> It is like water and ice:
> Apart from water, no ice,
> Outside living beings; no buddhas.[1]

Hakuin has pointed at something very significant here, the non-dual awakened perspective is available to all, but some people are trapped in ice. Their essences are frozen. Hakuin recommends meditation to thaw the ice.

If a person's essence, their consciousness energy, is frozen in the body, there is no flow. This makes it impossible for the person to feel the non-dual vast interconnectedness as it feels like their being is a frozen block of wood in the moment, a rock. Awakening is like water and then vapour, and if you are like frozen ice, this is impossible to feel. A person needs a melting of the ice. Countless times I have had others say to me that they are unable to feel any of the non-dual vast interconnectedness. This is not a surprise to me. They typically are totally frozen in their bodies, totally contracted around their body, frozen in misery and suffering. They need to melt and thaw out to get the process going. As therapist Miriam Greenspan explained, on working with energy and the dark emotions, "to let it go, you have to let it flow." [2]

Now, if a person is frozen in their essence, then the person can experience a deep loss of resourcefulness, a sense of numbness, a sense of feeling like a loser. This is hard to live with, but the person can end up coping by constructing a sense of identity of being a victim and a loser, a personal narcissistic gig. It goes like this: "I am special because I have been such a victim in my life. I have not had the breaks of other people, and I have constantly been screwed over by the system." This becomes a narcissistic gig which is not as readily apparent as other narcissistic gigs. This is like an underbelly narcissistic gig as it involves taking refuge in complaints, victimhood, and low self-esteem.

Chad's Underbelly Narcissism

Chad held on tightly to his victim stance. During a session, while working with him, he explained to me that he had never gotten a break his whole life. He was always being screwed over by the system, and now in his late forties he felt absolutely worthless. He had drifted through the mental health system, gone through addiction treatment for pot dependency, worked for a while, received disability payments, and then had changed his life by going to university and graduating with a social work degree. But instead of working in his career field after graduation, he returned to receiving disability payments. Three years later, he was sharing his long list of complaints with me. I looked over at him, and thought, *You're an underbelly narcissist.* But I knew I could not challenge him on that yet.

Chad was feeling numb, so I knew I had to get his energy flowing and circulating. Angry catharsis can be a good way to open somebody up especially if a person is feeling shut down. I asked him who are you really mad at. He looked at me, smiled:

" A lot of people, but the first person that comes up is you. I am angry at you because when I tried to line up counselling with you, you tried to set me up with one of your associates."

I smiled to myself, as it was true. "Yes Chad, I have a few people working with me as counsellors, and when you called the practice, I tried to see if one of them could take you on as I was very busy between the university teaching, writing, and my private practice and groups. How did that make you feel when I tried to refer you on to one of the other counsellors?"

"Hurt and angry," Chad said.

"Look into my eyes, and tell me how hurt and angry you were."

Chad sighed and said, "Screw you, Gary, for not taking me on as a client right away."

"Louder," I said. "Give it to me *hard*."

Chad stood up and yelled, "Screw you, Gary, for not seeing me right away."

"Use your arms," I said.

Suddenly with eyes bulging, Chad stood up, and with his right hand pointing intensely at me, Chad yelled at the top of his lungs, "*Fuck you, Gary!*" It felt like a primal scream that filled the room with vibrational intensity.

"Wonderful," I said to Chad. " Now sit back down in the chair, and enjoy the energy. Just be with whatever feelings that are coming up, with no judgment."

Chad sat down quietly in his chair. "I don't feel hurt as much as sad, but it feels different, softer, more spacious."

"Nice" I said to Chad. "That was cathartic. You screamed out some rage, and now you are more in the flow of energy. And here I want you to look at something."

He looked back at me curiously.

"In your own way, Chad," I said, "you have been caught in an underbelly narcissist stance against existence."

"What does that mean?"

I hesitated, in working with Chad, I could readily see that he was a seasoned hardened consumer of counsellor services in which he had heard it all before, so there was not much that could get his attention. So the only thing left for me was to keep on going with gusto.

"It is easy to see the narcissistic components of people caught up in the specialness of being number one, and trying to make the world their oyster. What is trickier to perceive is the narcissism of the person is who is claiming worthlessness, victimhood, and *loserhood*. Rather than living off positive self-representations and the validation of others to show how special they are, underbelly narcissists are caught in a whirlpool of negative self-talk, stories about the dirty rotten deal they are getting, and their so-called loserhood. But that too is a stance against existence."

"All of your stories and complaints," I said, "are just a way for you to hang onto your specialness, your persona of being the guy who has got no breaks and has been screwed by the system. The truth is you betrayed yourself a long time ago, although you pretended to be a rebel. You sold out your essence for this victim gig, and used it to justify to yourself why you stopped taking risks, and basically put yourself in the dugout of life, rather than going up to bat."

Chad looked dumfounded. He did not know what to think.

In a nutshell, I had just given him the essence of Almaas's transformation of narcissism approach.[3] A person has to see that the narcissistic gig has been an empty shell, a sense of being fake in which he or she has lived off the opinions of others to feel special and all of it has been very ordinary. Chad was not the first to think he was a misunderstood rebel screwed by the system, there were millions of others with the same deal. So, it was not special, but very ordinary. The essential thing, as Almaas stresses, is that a person needs to see that the "great betrayal" has not been done by others to self but by self to self. We have to see that we did it to ourselves, we sold out ourselves. So Chad needed to see that, although he had some hard blows and difficult situations to deal with, long ago he had sold his essence out for some black sheep persona and he has been complaining and caught in this loser gig ever since.

Chad looked over at me, and surprisingly said, "Gary you are right. I don't know what to say."

I invited him to just sit with this awareness in the moment.

"Just sit in the chasm of being, as narcissism drops away, and allow yourself to descend into your guts."

As he we sitting there, I said to him, "Join the club, I too, have been a complete narcissist."

We both laughed uproariously.

After our laughter, I looked over at Chad, and said, "Each of us has to find out that *I too have been the problem*. Now, just rest in being. You can feel vulnerable and open, but that is okay."

Chad smiled.

"Thank you for seeing me Gary, this has been quite the session. I need to go home and digest all of this."

We wrapped up our session soon after this. This day signalled a change for Chad. He now could see that he could drop directly into being and stop hanging onto his screwed-by-the-system, loser gig. The sailing was not always smooth after this, but it was a huge shift into beingness for Chad, and the process of dropping of stories and hanging onto negative labels had started.

Many of us do not get caught for long in the underbelly narcissist gig like Chad, but do nevertheless visit it from time to time. When this happens, I suggest some form of catharsis—directing energy out at an empty chair, or a tree in the woods, or some form of intense physical exercise, or meditation to regain the flow of energy. Follow this by just sitting in being in the moment, and see if all of the complaints, stories, and victim identity can all be dropped in the moment, as you rest in being.

CHAPTER 8
Addictive Rituals to Heal Inadequacy

I have covered the whole quest from addiction to non-dual being in my book *Beyond Addiction to Awakening*. In this chapter, I am not exploring the experience of being chronically stuck in grasping at some addictive ritual, whether it be a substance, another person, an activity, or the underlying addiction to ego and narcissism, or even the mind. Rather, here I am uncovering a more secret path. This is when a person is functioning, in many ways, at a beingness level, but at the same time has a secret life, in which he or she plunges into addictive behaviours. I have an international non-dual therapy practice, and I get calls, consultations, and requests for non-dual Skype sessions from people who are well established in the non-dual path, and who are sometimes working with well known teachers like Adyashanti and Mooji. However, in many cases they have a secret addiction which they have not been able to liberate through their non-dual understanding. In working with these individuals, I go back to the basics that I covered in *Beyond Addiction to Awakening*. This means we have to go back to sitting in our pain, learn to be non-judgmentally one with it, learn to allow our energy to flow, and then just be mindful of our grasping and cravings and return to the *what is* of the moment. We will see, in the following case study, how Terry had avoided the underlying pain of inadequacy and not feeling good enough, and instead sought a remedy through sexually acting out. He needed to re-realize that the healing path was through the pain itself.

Terry Learns to Sit in His Pain

Terry was an art therapist in his forties and been involved in the non-dual scene for many years. He had been in a series of relationships with females on and off again for many years. He would have a relationship for a while and then they would break up, and a few months later he would start a new relationship with another woman. This all sounded innocent enough until he explained to me that the complicating factor was that he had a secret other life in which, late at night, he would go to gay steam baths and have anonymous sex with a variety of men. He prided himself in that he always was the one receiving the oral sex and seemed fixated on the sense of power that he enjoyed in these encounters. He would even sometimes go out with a woman, and later that night, pretend to be kind of tired, drop her off at her house, and proceed to the steam baths. When a relationship with a woman would start to flourish, he would end up confessing what he was involved in because the woman would inevitably sense there was something going on and demand an explanation. Often, the woman would be quite devastated at first, but try to be understanding with assurances from Terry that his behaviour would stop, but on and he would go. He had tried to use his willpower to stop, but a few drinks and that was it, off he went for gay sex.

As we worked on this together, he told me about the many psychologists and sexual addiction groups he had been to and that nothing had worked. He reported that he would try the strategies for a while, make promises to stop and *draw a line in the sand*, but inevitably a few days or a few weeks later he would be back involved in the same behaviours. As we were talking, I sensed that he wanted more strategies, but I refused to supply him with any semblance of a hopeful strategy, and instead told him we were going to use a non-dual approach to this and totally work on this through awareness. We were going to go to the unwanted place, which he self-medicated himself out of with his sexual acting out. We were going to go to that place of dark pain to embrace acceptance. I asked him:

"So, just before you have your two drinks, followed by your acting out, how are you feeling?"

Terry paused for a minute. "I am feeling hopeless, and inadequate."

Bingo, I thought to myself.

"Have you ever sat in your feelings of inadequacy and hopelessness with no judgment?" I asked though I already knew the answer.

"No," he said.

Here, I decided to lay it out for him.

"So rather than just sitting in your feelings of hopelessness and inadequacy, and probably a general sense of being not good enough, at those times, you reject those feelings, by first having a couple of drinks, and then by going to the steam baths. Can you see that, in the moment, you are rejecting this moment for some better future moment through your addiction ritual, which is the heart of addiction. In effect you are saying to yourself, *Now is not okay, but if I do this, then I will be okay.* The tragic thing is that you are learning the habit of self-rejection in the moment. You need to turn this around."

With a smile Terry seemed to agree, so I decided to plunge into false core drivers as well.

Dissolving Terry's Emotions and False Core Drivers

Over the years, I discovered that there can be some crystallized thought forms attached to these deep dark emotions that must be looked at. Stephen Wolinsky describes how we need to become aware of false core drivers and false compensatory systems that have been at play in our deep emotions for the greater part of our life.[1] In explaining this to Terry I said:

"For example, let's look at the feeling of being inadequate. Now, if you sit in this feeling of inadequacy in this moment, what is the worst part about it?"

Terry stopped for a moment. "It makes me think I am unlovable."

By sitting in our worst experiences and feelings and simply by asking what is the worst part about this experience, we discover a core belief that we have inadvertently taken on and made central to our psychological system. Common examples of these statements are "I am worthless" –or– "I am bad" –or– "I am out of control" –or– "I am deficient" or as in Terry's case: "I am unlovable."

We lose our awareness of these core beliefs through what Wolinsky called our "false self compensator" which attempts to heal, transform, psychologically fix or use a spiritualized remedy in an attempt to overcome the false core. Tragically, our attempts to overcome the false core through our defensive systems only reinforces the false core because, at a deep level, we have accepted the false core foundation, we merely add material on top. Terry's running around, making these late night sexual connections had not healed the false core at all. Instead, Terry needed to slow down and be aware of these false core beliefs and let them dissolve by simply being mindful and present. The key here is that we have to sit in our false core directly and let it dissolve through non-judgmental awareness. So, I invited Terry to sit in his feeling of inadequacy and being unlovable right now in the session with no judgment, and let thoughts of inadequacy and being unlovable come up and do nothing about it, just sit in the feelings.

As Terry sat there over the next few minutes in his feelings, he was shocked. He had always thought the inadequacy feeling was too black to face, like tar that would swallow him whole, but as he sat with it with no judgment, something new started to happen for him. The black tar experience started to melt and become more spacious simply by being one with it. By not trying to do anything with it, but just being one with the feelings of inadequacy, healing was happening. In fact, after a few minutes, inadequacy started to feel something very different.

"Like a spacious sadness," he said.

I laughed. "Now it has become like a deep broken-hearted sadness which is poignant but okay, almost like a beautiful sad song."

Inadequacy was revealing itself as a broken-hearted sadness—how touching. And in this place, Terry found his sense of being unlovable had transformed to a loving tenderness. So here Terry was learning to accept the dark emotion and befriend and surrender to it, rather than striving to attack it and move away from it.

Staying in Awareness: Watching the Craving

To carry on with the second part of my intervention, I reminded Terry that the non-dual path always focuses on staying in awareness no matter what. I gave the following example:

"Have you ever noticed that when you are drinking, you may keep going until the curtain of your conscious awareness starts to come down, and despite that, you keep drinking even though you are starting to become unconscious?"

"Totally," Terry said. "I do that all the time, drink some wine, start becoming unconscious, and then decide to go out for some steam bath sex."

Terry had laid the pattern out nicely; he had allowed himself to go unconscious.

"You need to make an agreement with me," I said. "From this point on, that no matter what you always stay in your awareness, you are always conscious of what is going on."

Terry tried to argue with me that this would be hard, but I reminded him it only took one moment at a time to be aware. Seeing this, he agreed to my proposition that he stay in his awareness no matter what. So, I moved to the cravings part.

"Now what I want you to do is, when you are feeling down, or hopeless, or inadequate, sit in your feelings with awareness, and then watch how a craving will arise in consciousness which says *do this* to make yourself feel better. In short, a craving will arrive. But instead of grabbing onto it, just be watchful of it, allow it to arise and then fall away. You do not have to act on it. And even if you do, stay in your awareness. So that means, even if you have a couple of drinks, and top that off with going to the steam baths, stay in your awareness no matter what."

My invitation seemed innocent enough for Terry, so he readily agreed. I wrapped up our session with that as that seemed enough for him. Sitting in his dark emotions, staying in awareness and watching his cravings was him homework.

Awareness: A Fire that Burns Addiction

When I followed up with Terry a month later, he reported that he had been okay, in that he had only one relapse in a month, while previous to this he had been going to the steam baths on a regular weekend basis. When I asked him what happened, he said:

"Even when I did act out, it was different because I could already feel the hopelessness of the cycle going into it. The release was far better in my fantasy then actual reality, and I was shocked at how fast I was back in the feeling of hopelessness and inadequacy, literally moments after sex. It is like the hopelessness of the whole cycle seemed to be there all of the time. And it seemed crazy because, that night, I drank three glasses of wine, and it seemed that I was losing my awareness anyways, and could not even really enjoy the acting out because I was almost too drunk. So, it seems the whole cycle is based on me being somewhat unconscious. And after I acted out, in the next couple of weeks, the feeling of inadequacy would come up, and instantly a craving would be there for anonymous sex, but I said to myself, *what is the point? I am just going to feel worse afterwards.* So I just stayed with the feeling of inadequacy. So it seems, a whole bubble is being burst just through awareness."

I followed up by asking him how did sitting in his dark emotions go? He said he had made it a regular practice every night of sitting in dark feelings of hopelessness and inadequacy every night for fifteen minutes and soon found himself realizing that these emotions were just energy. *Nice,* I thought to myself. He also said he had a Saturday group that got tripped up by one of the attendees being somewhat manic and upstaging him, and normally he might have come home and had a few glasses of wine and then go act out, but this time he just sat in his upset sense of things and what a fuck-up it all was. And, within a few minutes, he was laughing because, though he could feel the loss, he could also see the humour of the whole situation. He did not have to get mired in inadequacy. He just let it be there and expand into a heartfelt vulnerability and recognition of the fact that he is not in control and sometimes things go astray. He could be sad that the group went off the rails, and that was okay.

As we were talking, I could feel Terry's relief.

"What we are doing is bringing your non-dual understanding to *all of you,* even the unwanted, the dark emotions and the hidden rituals of addiction. Your sexual acting out has been a gift of transformation for you as, even here through awareness, you find a deepening of your non-dual understanding."

We both just sat together and enjoyed the non-dual perfection of what is, even relating to a path of secretly acting out.

CHAPTER 9
Escaping Nothingness

There is a tragic stuckness when a person may have started the journey into awakening with some zest but becomes frightened as he or she encounters nothingness or the emptiness of existence. In short, the person has an experience of falling into the abyss, but not completely. The apparent individual starts tuning into existence and starts feeling the vast emptiness of existence. The world collapses into emptiness and their ego gets caught fighting the void and can not handle the vast abyss of emptiness and the prospect of letting go of self. In the end, the person becomes so frightened and pulls away and retreats in one way or another back into the familiar ground of the dualistic world of the ego.

The problem with escaping the abyss of nothingness is, as the saying goes, *everywhere you go, there you are*—you take nothingness with you. So, once nothingness starts opening inside you, escaping through some strategy psychological or spiritual will only temporarily resolve the issue, in that it has not been fully worked out. In the following case example, we will see that escaping is not a true resolution of the issue.

Bill's Begging and Praying out of the Abyss

Let me give you a specific example. There was a bright financial advisor Bill, who attended some of my non-dual group therapy sessions for about one year. He was a fan of western existential philosophers such as Kierkegaard and Sartre and was also a Christian. He complained that he was feeling a lot of meaningless and emptiness in his life despite being a very successful professional and having a longterm marriage.

In group one day, I invited him just to settle into this meaninglessness and emptiness that he was always talking about. I invited him to not think about it, but just be in his body to feel the emptiness and meaninglessness—to just sink into it. As I gave him these instructions, I watched his face as he let go into the emptiness. He started to relax into it, but then I could see in his eyes and body that he was feeling a lot of fear. I asked him what is going on.

"My god," he said. "This emptiness is too much. I am afraid I am going to be swallowed up in it."

I thought this was a good sign. He was really getting into it.

"Just become one with the emptiness," I said. "Give up your struggle, make no judgment."

I could tell immediately that these instructions were something Bill could not follow. He resisted them.

"I have to do something," he said. "I am going to go mad."

All of a sudden something changed for Bill. I saw his lips moving, and his energy change. I just let him sit in that for a few minutes, and then I asked him what was going on for him.

"It was horrible," he said. "I could not stand it, so I started to pray to Jesus, and Jesus was there for me, and now everything is okay."

Even more than that, as I looked over at him, he seemed to feel a little smug. Then he said to me, "I would like to leave it at that for today."

I had no choice but to leave it at that with Bill. He had aborted his emptiness through prayer, and did not allow a non-dual experience to set in because, in fear, he desperately prayed to Jesus. The problem is that he is still caught carrying the nothingness deep within him. Out of fear, he started to pray to Jesus and so did not surrender to the emptiness. Instead of entering into this huge level of nothingness and emptiness opening up in his being, he managed it through prayer. He stopped coming to the non-dual group about a month later, never to return.

This case study points to a common problem in dealing with what Heidegger called the nothingness that opens up in the near-side of being.[1] Many people start to plunge into nothingness but find it too awesome and terrorizing and retreat from it with one sort of management strategy or another. The problem, though, is that nothingness and emptiness is here to stay. It is eternal. It is a part of existence, and it is always going to keep coming back. The mistake made is that we try to manage the nothingness with our ego.

The invitation here is not to retreat from this all encompassing nothingness and emptiness even though it can feel very scary and overwhelming. If one can learn to sit in this emptiness, with no judgment, and become one with the emptiness, to our shock, we can find that it is not a negative nothingness but a vibrant intense emptiness: a *full* emptiness. The paradox is that, what looks like an unbearable experience, ends up being an ecstatic emptiness that is all encompassing and translucent. We just have to stay in choiceless awareness and let go of the self.

Stalled Nothingness: Back to the Convenience Store

There is even a stranger pattern I have noticed in working with a whole range of people on their non-dual journey over the years, and that is when a person appears to have quite a significant opening and awakening into non-dual being and yet, after a few months, drifts back into a previous sedate consciousness. I call this going back to a *7-11 convenience store* existence. It is a total shock to me how somebody who appears to be radiating the light of existence can drift back into almost a sedate non-risk-taking settled existence.

Rory was like that. He had experienced some huge awakenings into non-dual consciousness. Upon graduating from university, he took a counselling job up in a northern remote area of Canada with long, cold winters. He spent the next ten years primarily hanging out with his clients and settled into a sedate existence watching endless television at night in his cabin and working with the community by day. When he came to a non-dual conference after being in hiatus for ten years, he was shocked by how much he had lost the non-dual edge compared to some of his non-dual friends he had graduated with. Being on cruise control does nothing for the non-dual energy. In fact, the connection slowly fritters away if the person is not honouring the living light of the absolute radiating through them. What we give our attention to day-in and day-out is what we become, and Rory's attention was given to appreciation of a laid back lifestyle in which he thought he had it made due the lack of demands put on him. I have noticed that, if a person stops taking risks in the day-to-day aspect of living, it impacts the non-dual energy flowing through them; it is almost like the person becomes a hoarder—rather than a sharer—of energy. Rory was like that, a hoarder, and it showed. What possessed him to stop radiating the energy with intensity? He went back to a non-risk, convenience existence.

The Imagination Escape

We have seen that a total embrace of the void—transforming it into a full emptiness—can be aborted prior to taking the requisite leap, or it can be stalled out afterwards. I have also noticed another interesting escape from the total self-annihilation of the person as the vast nothingness of existence is embraced. It is the problem that Ouspensky called the *imagiazone* which is a similar term to Gurdjieff's term *kundabuffer*.[2] Here the problem is that the imagination of the mind of the person takes over whether it is with kundalini experiences or the signs of awakening. The mind can be wonderful at using creative imagination to recapture the details of the experience.

Norma was a counsellor in her late twenties who had some powerful awakening experiences to the non-dual but seemed to have a little trouble dealing with the ultimate darkness and the threat of non-existence. She never could relax with choiceless awareness and no-judgment into the experience of non-being and non-existence. Her mind would get in the way and come up with powerful images of what was going on. The problem was that these were images that had stuck in her through poems and paintings, and she would seize on these images and spend a lot of time analyzing them. The attraction was that some of these poems and drawings were captivating and moving, and she would get lots of positive feedback about them.

Over time, the poems, writings, and drawings became a barrier to embracing the vast darkness of existence that was showing up in her life. Working with me, she once again had to let all of these images go, and just sit in what I would call the dark-side-of-the-moon energy of total absence and non-existence, all with no judgment even though it literally terrified her out of her mind. Sitting together with Norma, she was able to do that: sit in the ultimate blackness and make no effort to save herself, and not look to her mind for a remedy but just to sit in this ultimate darkness. Despite her terror, it only took about thirty seconds for her to relax into the shadow of death and feel the energy change from total terror to the vastness of existence. Images and words could not save her here. All had to be dropped so she could be one with the darkest place, non-existence. But to her amazement, she found she was one with this energy, and she was part of the non-existent night of existence from which everything emerged from. It was a beautiful shift of energy. As we wrapped up our session, I invited Norma to continue to sit in this place of non-being and enjoy the serene relaxation of it.

CHAPTER 10
Losing Motivation: Running on Empty

The trouble is that, when we are caught up in the dream of getting somewhere, we are perpetual strivers who are constantly *doing* something. We are never at rest. You hear people say that with a great deal of pride: "I am a doer." We may not even know where we are going, but we are determined that we are going somewhere.

However, over time, we can start running out of gas. As we grow exhausted from striving, everything starts to appear meaningless and trivial, and now we are definitely in the grey zone. All of our goals seem worthless, and the things that use to keep us going, like advanced degrees and promotions, all start to seem pointless. The sense of running out of personal resources or having no will or motivation is a sign that the so-called *personal self* is running out of steam. This can be terribly threatening to the person who, up to now, was driven and always striving. Motivation is reached for and there is nothing there, the gas tank is empty. Now the person feels aimless and lost. Ego motivation is gone. The abyss of nothingness swallows everything up including ego-based motivation, leaving the striver in a state of enervation. It is like they are running on fumes.

It is a fertile opportunity, to find ourselves lost and with no motivation. It represents a transition point from personal ego projects to surrendering to existence and turning will over to the absolute.

We will see from the following case study, the only way to work this through is to accept the lostness and unmotivated state with no judgment and plunge into nothingness by resolving the gap between the illusionary "I" and the nothingness itself. In short, a person has to *be* the nothingness without resistance and learn to let existence flow through and be open to the absolute will of existence. One now is a conduit. Almaas calls it discovering the diamond will.[1]

Carly Learns To Follow Her Bliss

Carly was psychologist who had worked her way up at a local agency after graduate school, and now, as she began to explore her own non-dual journey in earnest, she could feel herself becoming attuned to something deep inside, which she had always felt nagging away at her. She had never felt as though she fit in, for there was always a gnawing sense of being an outsider, and she longed to arrive somewhere that mirrored back at her a sense of belonging. And now, as she started to embrace her being and give up the mirage of the ego, something else huge happened. She had always been a striver, in her words: "I always have to be doing something." And now all of that was suddenly falling away. She got a promotion to a supervisory position at the agency she worked at, and she felt nothing. Here she was in her late forties, exactly where she had thought wanted to be, and it meant nothing to her. Being a success as a health professional, getting promoted, and having the respect of her peers did not matter. Carly found herself falling into the abyss, and all the usual striving and motivation was gone. She consulted me for a session.

As we started our work together, it was immediately clear that Carly was very concerned with how lost she was. I laughed to myself. Being lost is only apparently bad if you judge it to be so—we are all beings lost in eternity. As Carly was already falling into nothingness, I invited us to plunge into nothingness right in our session. Carly said she was absolutely terrified but that she would go along with it, for terror had been something she had been feeling a lot these days. So, right there in the moment, I said to Carly:

"I want you to relax into the nothingness that pervades everything and that you feel inside you right now. But this time, I want you to close the gap, and realize that you are the nothingness, and there is nothing you can do about it."

I could see by Carly's rapid eye-movement, even with her eyes closed, that she was still having trouble, so I followed up with some more instructions:

"Now as you are sitting in nothingness, remember: no judgment, stay in no-judgment. And as you are sitting in no-judgment, give up any attempt to save yourself, just be with the nothingness."

This seemed to make an immediate difference as I could feel Carly relaxing into the nothingness, out of her head into her belly. A serene smile started to come over Carly. I asked Carly in her serene state what was going on.

"I just feel the vastness," she said, "and it has a beautiful blue light to it."

"Just stay with that," I said. "Enjoy."

She just sat there for a few minutes, until I could see her eyes flickering, so I asked her what is going on.

"My mind was asking how to keep this going without thought," she said.

We both laughed at the hilarity of the mind asking how to go beyond itself.

"Just be in one moment at a time," I said, "and, when mind comes in notice it, and let it fall away."

Carly retuned into a reverie for a few more minutes and then we debriefed.

"Oh my god," Carly said. "I am okay even without motivation in the moment, as I am just the vast nothingness which feel serene and blissful."

I looked over at her. "So Carly, you can function from this vast nothingness, one moment at a time. And notice from this place you have no ego, but you have all of the energy of the absolute coming through you. You have lost your personal will, but now you have the absolute coming through you."

Carly could see this very clearly and was bubbling with excitement. "I know what I need to do. I can start moving my clients beyond narrative therapy to burning through all stories to be one with existence."

As it seemed exciting to me, I reminded her of Joseph Campbell's expression which seemed so resonant with her situation:

"You are following your bliss."[2]

Our session wrapped up for the day, but it was clear that Carly had made the transition from feeling lost in her lack of personal motivation, to embracing nothingness and letting the absolute sweep through her. She was excited. Her personal gas tank had become empty, but now she had all of the energy of the absolute running through her to rely on.

PART THREE
Hanging On: The Realm of the Blues

We believe in our perspective of separateness, and we try to resolve it by looking to the other to save us. Rather than trading one relationship for another or even looking for an awakening experience outside of ourselves, we need to heal this basic belief in separateness directly. All of our self–other object relations that we internalize can only be let go of if we can see through the belief in our own objective self. Once that belief in self is let go, the discrete separateness of others and so-called objective experience easily dissolves. The problem is that we all have learned at an early age to grasp at and expect nourishment from the other to fill our internal holes inside. This persistence in hoping the other can take you all the way home, even to awakening, is such an ingrained habit that to let it go makes us confront our deep inner void. Accepting inner emptiness, with nothing to hang or no other to define ourselves with, is the transformational invitation.

CHAPTER 11
Clinging to the Sanctuary of the Other

We can have a vague feeling about the existence of holes within but not really want to take a look at them directly and fill them up with essence by being one with them, for it is too frightening. Where do these dark holes come from? Almaas described them as coming mostly from childhood:

> These holes originated during childhood, partly as a result of traumatic experiences or conflicts with the environment. Perhaps your parents did not value you. They didn't treat you as if your wishes or presence were important, didn't act in ways that let you know that you mattered. They ignored your essential value. Because your value was not seen or acknowledged (perhaps even attacked or discouraged), you got cut off from that part of you, and what was left was a hole, a deficiency.[1]

As we move into adulthood, we bring our wounds from childhood. Firman and Gila asked a group of addictions counsellors to imagine what were they feeling just before they had the urge to use alcohol or drugs. Here is the list they came up with:

Disintegration
Worthlessness
Lost
Disconnection
Lack of existence
Invisible
Bad
Evil
Void
Vacuum
Abandoned
Alone
Powerless
Wimpy
Wrong
Tense
Paranoid
Not breathing, nonbeing
Humiliated
Shame
Unloved [2]

We have all such wounds, which we try to medicate with some type of addictive process. We can compound these dark emotional wounds with our own basic wound of separation in which we moved from essence into separation and ego. We abandon our being as little children to survive with our parents, siblings and friends. We are left with a disconnected being with a variety of additional emotional wounds. All of these dark emotions need to be worked through directly. See Miriam Greenspan's *Healing The Dark Emotions* about the process of becoming one with the emotion, surrendering and letting the energy flow.[3] The essential process is to become one with the emotion with no judgment, honour what needs to be done at the physical level, and just let the energy flow through, reclaiming essence in the process.

However, rather than healing the dark emotions directly, many of us choose an addictive remedy for instant relief. In a previous chapter on split-off addiction, we explored how people can have secret addiction rituals to deal with dark, uncomfortable feelings. In this chapter, we explore the very common addictive remedy of relying on another person to help with these dark emotional states. We get the other person to help fill these emotional wounds, these black holes. In short, we start to be co-dependent, as we begin to depend on other people to fill these holes. Our holes get filled with what we believe we're getting from the other person. Almaas described a poignant example relating to feeling valued:

> For example, you may feel valued because this person appreciates you. You don't know consciously that you're filling the hole with their appreciation. But when you are with that person, you feel valuable, and unconsciously you feel the other person is responsible for your value. Whatever this person is giving you feels like a part of you; it is part of the fullness that you experience.[4]

There are, of course, problems as no one person can fill all of our holes. Also, other people may change and not fill the holes in the way they use to. Or there can be a loss of someone who has been very close and intimate, and all of a sudden we are right back feeling the deficiency and the emptiness and the worthlessness that we had filled with the other person's love and valuing. We can then become very defensive against feeling the loss and the hole directly as we do not want to get in touch with the magnitude of the emptiness or the feeling that something is wrong with us at a core level.

The process for healing is to stop being defensive and just learn to sit in the experience of these holes, feel the absence of essence, and then, through presence and attunement, let essence naturally and spontaneously fill and heal the hole. This process can be challenging. As we work on the holes, they can appear to get bigger and bigger until one day it becomes apparent that there is a need to work on the big black hole of death, which is sitting in the middle of all of this.

The process can even become more complicated as we realize that we have not only used loved ones to fill our holes. As well, when we began our spiritual pursuits, we started using spiritual teachers and mentors to fill our holes. To heal our hole of being, we looked to be saved by the "Other." It is an enacting of the central object relation between the central ego and the ideal other, which we look to in order to be comforted, satisfied, fulfilled, and nourished. We started this pattern early on with our mothers who we looked at to tell us how wonderful we were and to nourish and bless us and take care of our needs. From there it went to father, to teachers, and coaches and mentors. The problem is that we can carry this pattern on with a spiritual teacher or spiritual mentor. We use this special other to be taken care of, to be nourished, to be special, and to have our awakening or enlightenment path delivered to us. This connection can be a way of soothing our selves at a deep level, and it is something that we have been doing with the idealized other since we were little. And the sad part about this pattern is that it may be, for the most part, unconscious.

Now I have had the privilege of working with all sorts of seekers who have been closely working with the who's who of non-dual teachers from Papaji to Osho to Trungpa to J. Krishnamurti to Nisargadatta to Balsekar to Adyashanti to Gangaji to Mooji—the list goes on. Now some of these people have been going from one teacher to the next for twenty, thirty and forty years. There seems to be a lack of awareness of the fact that all of this externalized seeking for non-dual awakening through the idealized other is an avoidance of the big black hole of being within.

There comes a point when a person needs to realize that relying on another is merely an obstruction. The question becomes, after so many years: has that strategy of relying on somebody else to take you to awakening *worked*? Or really, as J. Krishnamurti always pointed out in his anti-guru stance, have you used the other to avoid seeing and being in the desperateness of your own situation. You thought you had found a path, but actually you are lost as ever as you have never seen into your own true nature. You never embraced your own path directly as you have avoided plunging into your own black hole by grasping onto a teacher. We have wanted techniques and methods from the idolized other to avoid sitting in our own lostness and black hole directly.

Wanting the shortcut to awakening, we want to get there the fastest way possible. So, we get pulled into asking for techniques and guidance. The problem, however, is that awakening is a seeing and understanding beyond time and causality, but we want to make it predictable and formulaic. We need to see if, in all our techniques and admiration of our spiritual teacher, we have not moved an inch. We may have felt soothed and our specialness guaranteed by the wondrous other. Yet, the invitation is to see through this deceptive pattern and let go of reliance on the other and sit in the hopelessness of being in which our own black hole is sat in directly. We embrace existence from here, where we have been at all the way along but have been too frightened to look and be in.

We can be lazy. I know I was. I thought Osho could just lay it all out, and I did not have to figure it all out myself. But I had to confront my own laziness and my own sense of being on a special path, particularly with the sense of wonderment I got from listening to and reading Osho discourses. I had to see it is really just a form of begging for nourishment, specialness and affirmation. It was like I was just trying to grab awakening through the light of the guru.

This strategy, of course, was doomed for failure, for awakening is not an experience but an understanding at a total being-level, something that has to be realized and not imitated.

As I relaxed my demand on the idealized other to spiritually save me and sweep me to enlightenment, it allowed me to deepen my own understanding beyond the idealized other. I saw that there were actually no spiritual teachers as nobody is awakened, or 'only nobodies are awakened', and a whole deconstruction process occurred. Awakening is not, after all, a personal thing, it is simply tuning into an awakened existence. Awakened beings, no matter how grand they appear, are actually just nobodies: nobodies inviting nobodies to realize they are nobody. To see awakening as the simple realization that there is no separate self here completely demystifies the whole process. It takes the throne away from all the spiritual teachers and gurus. The open secret is that it is all available to us right here, right now. There is no such thing as an inner sanctuary or a privileged few. The invitation is in this moment. No amount of meditation or effort or discipline is necessary to recognize who I already am in this moment. It merely takes a seeing or recognition right here, right now.

The Romantic Other: "I Need Your Love"

It would not be fair to leave this chapter on letting go of the other, without some exploration of the whole issue of looking for a romantic partner. What is interesting is that often, a person can have clarity that no spiritual teacher is the answer and that the idealized guru or spiritual teacher cannot save him or her, yet they may have a total lack of clarity about the quest for a romantic relationship. In short, it is almost like the person wants to be saved by the love from the romantic other. Here, again we really see the acting out of the central object relation as described by Almaas:

> So the central object relation integrates all of the good experiences you've had. You feel supported, loved, nourished, and wanted. It is the most basic object relation, the one you've engaged all of your life…The central object relation is a relationship between the central ego—the core or the central part of the soul—and what is called the ideal object or the ideal other. The object here is ideal in the sense that the object—the parent or the teacher or the teaching or the school or the breast, whatever it may be—is comforting, satisfying, fulfilling, nourishing, supporting, and giving.[5]

Now there is no more satisfying central object relation then the loving romantic boyfriend or girlfriend or spouse. People crave and long for that type of love. As Byron Katie would say, the central story tied up in it is "I need your love."[6] This can be a particularly female issue, although recently many counsellors are telling me this pattern of looking for the idealized love from a romantic partner is really showing up in males in their twenties and thirties.

Terra was in her thirties and had a successful professional life as an accountant. She had gone through many romantic relationships but no ongoing enduring one. Her story was that she needed a romantic relationship to be whole, and that there must be something wrong with her because she did not have a long-term relationship in her life. I invited her, in our therapeutic work together, to look at that story: "I need a long term romantic partner to be happy."

I used the first two of Byron Katie's four questions approach: "Is that true? Really, is that absolutely true?" At first Terra said it was true, but when I asked her if it was absolutely true, she laughed and said no it was not absolutely true that she needed romantic love to be happy.

I followed up with Byron Katie's third question: "What is it like when you believe that story about needing a romantic relationship to be happy?"

"I get self critical," she said. "I think something must be wrong with me, I get a little depressed."

"What's it like to drop that story?" I said, asking the fourth question.

Terra smiled. "I feel relaxed, happy, okay."

For homework, I had Terra agree to watch when this story comes up and not buy into it—to instead *deconstruct* the story.

"Don't grab the story and run with it, and get all miserable. Let it go right there in the moment," were my instructions.

As we were winding up, Terra said something very interesting, "I can see how this story about needing a romantic relationship got tied up with my non-dual awakening because I thought there must be something wrong with me if I don't have a romantic relationship, and if there is something wrong with me, non-dual awakening won't happen."

We both laughed, as that recognition of the binding impact of the story that "something was wrong with me" was huge. She could just let the story go. She could be open to a romantic relationship, but she did not *need* to have it.

Life is a vast interconnectedness in which aloneness and connection can be embraced and enjoyed. The joy of romantic connection can be celebrated, but when we decide we absolutely need it, we get into trouble. It always comes back to touch and let go, enjoy the connection in this moment but be in a place of let go, so one is open to whatever emerges in the next moment.

CHAPTER 12
Death of a Loved One:
An Invitation to Accept Our Own Death

As we explore the realm of the blues, one challenge that can shake us to our core is dealing with the death of a loved one—a death that we just cannot accept as that other person seems fundamental to our life as we know it. Here, we find the blue realm merging with black. I remember when my own twin brother died in his sleep five years ago, through an overdose of booze and prescription medication, it was not a shock to me because through the previous five years he had drifted from being a hard working lawyer family man to a "booze hound" consumer of wine, escort services and cocaine. He'd lost his job as a lawyer, his family, and social connections, and spent his last days drinking wine and reading the newspaper. He had cycled through treatment programs, even staying in one for sixty days, but was back drinking hard even on the plane back to his hometown. He had thrashed me a few times on the phone with drunken dark rage, and our encounters became few and far between. He was living a life of descending to death, a slow suicide. He had a choice of booze and death or a new life of recovery, and he chose what he was familiar with, booze. Even though it was a slow decline to death, it was still in its own way tragic.

At some point a couple years earlier, I had to let go of my efforts to help my brother as he was dragging me to hell with him, and so I just stayed present when he called. I let go of stories of the way it should be, and stayed in no judgment. A couple of days after he died, I remember standing in front of his open coffin and looked at his body at the funeral home. I was struck by the tragic sadness, and yet there was a strange sense of renewal in death. It was strangely okay—his death playing out the way it did. His energy was now back with the whole.

Some of us, however, have to deal with deaths where we get mired in a sense of *this shouldn't have happened*. Shirley was like that in dealing with the death of her father, and we will now turn to her case, in which we see that eventually death must be met head on for full healing to take place.

Watching Her Father Die: Recognizing Her Own Death

Shirley, in her thirties, came to see me for psychotherapy reporting that she was stuck in grief. We previously had worked together in a number of sessions focusing on surrender, choiceless awareness and no judgment. Her father had died of cancer about two years ago, before his 60th birthday, and she had never really come to terms with it. She was even at home with him when he died, but somehow she still felt very stuck. In the two years since, she had tried to let go and accept his death, but around and around she went. She was mad at existence for taking her best friend away. Before reconnecting with me, had she tried grief therapy, trauma therapy, mindfulness, existential therapy, but nothing seemed to work. We even had a couple of non-dual sessions together a year earlier working on choiceless awareness and surrender, but she had been still looking for a technique for all the pain to go away. Now, here she was, still caught missing her dad, and with the perceived injustice of him dying early in his life. *Sixty is not old,* she thought. Shirley was unsure if I could do anything to help her. She was desperately hopeful that something would work.

As we sat down together, and Shirley recounted her pain and grief, she was looking at me with pleading eyes, looking for some hopeful strategy. Unfortunately, I could not provide any such hope. I had to go straight to the heart and assist her to see that her father's death was an invitation for her to accept her own death.

With a sigh, for I was about to lead her into the treacherous place of being out at sea with no life jacket and no help for hundreds of miles around, I said to her:

"You need to embrace the art of dying yourself, not just for your dad, but for you. You need to surrender to death. In short, you need to be without judgment or effort to escape, just allow yourself to die… just go down quietly."

I stopped with that and just let that sink in.

Shirley seemed perplexed. "How am I suppose to do that?"

I smiled. "Using a technique or working with me would not be surrender. I can not do surrender for you. You have to do it all by yourself. You need to realize that there is nothing you can do to save yourself. You are screwed. Just accept that. Give up."

Shirley sat there puzzled, waiting for the next thing from me. But there was not another thing. She was expecting a long drawn out session, but I did something that day I rarely do, I cut the session short and wound it up. I told her that we had done this surrender work together before, but because I was doing it with her and for her, it was not total surrender. Today, I could actually do nothing to help her surrender, any further help from me would be an avoidance. I just left her with the invitation of surrender and giving up all on her own. It was going to be the flight of the alone to the alone.

As we wound up the session, and she left, I could tell Shirley was confused. In her mind, it was like she was saying, *What type of counselling is this?* I did nothing, as I did not want to take her dilemma away. I let her leave. Shirley later told me she was, in fact, mad. But then she went home, and sat with things. It took a while, but in the silence of the wee hours of the morning, she got to that place of absolute aloneness and hopelessness, in which she realized there was nothing she could do, and she just gave up trying to save herself. She let go and went down quietly. She reported, at that point, it actually was serene and only took a few minutes.

Strange, she thought. She had avoided the helpless and hopelessness of surrendering into the blackness of death for two years, and here she had done it only in a fifteen minutes. And as she sat there in the eternal stillness of 2 a.m. in the darkness of night, she felt the wonderful transcendent silence of existence as the blackness transformed all by itself into a radiant translucent aliveness. With accepting the reality of her own death, and feeling the vastness of existence, suddenly there was acceptance of her father's death as well.

Shirley went on to explore many more things in her journey, but she found this acceptance experience to be pivotal. She was abiding in no judgment and in the acceptance of her own death. She realized that death is already inside of us all of the time, life and death merged in the intensity of this moment, and her father's death was a natural part of the ebb and flow of existence. He had returned to the formless.

CHAPTER 13
Waiting for Lightning to Strike

Waiting for the other can take on the pattern of waiting for an enlightenment experience, and this is a slippery pattern. It is subtle and can be quite deceptive. People can slip into a perpetual waiting mode for years, even decades. They typically report some variation of, *I am waiting for something to happen.* They want some big event, some huge awakening experience as a signpost of awakening. To loosen up our stance, I use the metaphor of it is like a person is "waiting for god" to show up, and I like to call this "waiting for Godot" from the Samuel Beckett play in which two characters, Vladamir and Estragon, are wait endlessly for the arrival of the mysterious Godot.[1]

The problem though is that existence is already here, everything is already available. We do not have to get to there, it is already here. All waiting entails a gap, a person is waiting for awakening but existence is always already here. The waiting implies a waiter and a separate existence, that is two, I and thou, but non-dual being happens when there is not two, the I gives way so existence can reveal itself.

Waiting implies the mind is still seeking. The mind is still hungry and seeking something. The mind is still future oriented, and looking for some goal of salvation in the future, waiting for some lightning enlightenment experience in the future. This demand for a wondrous enlightenment experience is the ultimate in desire. The seeker is looking for some fantastic awakening experience like the Buddha apparently had under the bodhi tree. This waiting is a set-up and can go on forever.

Over the last number of years, I have had the opportunity to work with people who have been waiting for awakening for decades. When I work with them, no matter what path they have been on from Tibetan Buddhism, to working with Osho, to working with Adyashanti, I have to point out one obvious thing, and that is with all of their seeking and waiting for decades they actually have not moved an inch. All of this seeking has been a grand illusion, as here they are still stuck in this moment. I am always surprised though, for they do not want to hear this; they want to hear some new strategies for more seeking. They end up feeling quite thunderstruck when I point out to them that there is nowhere to go and nothing to do as it is all available right here, right now, and it has been available all the way along. It is hard for a person to let that in, because then it seems like thirty years of seeking has just been flushed down the toilet. But, I like to say to the person:

"All of this was necessary to help you ripen. You have been able to ripen and swallow this bitter pill and embrace that in all your seeking you have not moved an inch."

Further to this, seeing that a person has not actually moved an inch, is debunking the illusion of spiritual progress. The whole illusion of gradual progress is a huge cosmic joke. There is no nice way to say this: what is needed is a giving up, a letting go, a surrender to "just this." This realization of the wisdom of non-attainment means it is seen that one can't get slowly closer to "just this", for it is a sudden realization, a relaxation, a letting go of effort, for it is seen that it is all available, right here, right now. Even on the path of gradual awakening, you have taken steps all the way up to what you think is the top of the platform, you still will have to jump off the staircase of effort at the very end. If one has to do it at the very end of gradual awakening, why not do it straight away?

The problem with the illusory gradual path is that you are *managing* and making deals and begging all the way up, for it all based on hope for the future, the Promised Land. In my own experience, I became exhausted with perpetual seeking and expectations, and I began to see that it could go on forever. Resolution came through an out of control falling, and bottoming out into "just this." Exhaustion itself took me down. There was no fight, no strategy, just a realization that the gig was up and an *unceremonious* falling to the ground. It was beautiful because there was no will involved.

It seems, however, people hang onto their illusion of waiting because they do not want to let in the absolute hopelessness of their stuck-in-waiting mode. It is like they have become so used to being on the sidelines of existence that they are content waiting there and moaning and complaining about how it has not happened to them yet. If there still is a self there, it will never happen. But it can be quite a nice pastime, a huge hobby, reading non-dual books, going to retreats, listening to discourses, chatting with friends, keeping a journal. It can keep a person nicely engaged for decades, all the time a person is waiting, with a plethora of mind explanations and hopeful new strategies.

With people stuck in this waiting path, I always recommend a little insight mantra, and that is "now or never." This helps them tune in because it helps them realize that, when they tune in, it will be in the now, just like this moment, so why not *right* now? It intensifies their process. Now we will turn to look at an actual case.

Brad's Long Term Waiting

Often, in our waiting for lightning to strike, there can be an obvious issue of avoidance tied up with this strategy. Brad had been a counsellor and non-dual seeker for over thirty years. He had done the tour through Nisargadatta, Papaji, Gangaji, and lately was spending a lot of time going to retreats with Mooji. He had called me up because he had read my articles on transformation at the end of the line and somehow he felt it applied to him. As we were talking, he shared with me that he had a wonderful wife of forty years, but no kids. And now that he was semi-retired. He found himself feeling lonely, exhausted and useless, just seeing a few clients a week. The day before he talked to me, he had signed up for another two week retreat in Europe with Mooji.

As Brad and I were talking, it became obvious to me that he did not see how his fear of his own loneliness—he had just turned seventy—was tied in to his pursuit of chasing Mooji around the world for retreats and waiting for enlightenment to strike. I asked him:

"What would it be like for you to sit in your loneliness, with no judgment?"

"I have never actually tried," he said.

I laughed to myself. Thirty years of seeking and chasing non-dual teachers around the world and Brad had never actually sat in his own loneliness. I gave him the invitation to sit in his own loneliness with no judgment as homework for him. He shakily agreed to do it.

When we skyped the next week, he had some surprising results to share with me. He had always avoided his loneliness or had tried to conquer it, but in the last week, he had just gone down to the beach by his house and rested on a bench and sat in his loneliness. At first, a lot of judgments came up about his loneliness, how awful he was, how old he was, how useless he was, but as he sat in no judgment and just let each judgment go as it came up, he had a sudden realization as his loneliness seemed to transform and become spacious.

"Loneliness is just energy," he said.

I mirrored back to him that was a huge insight.

Going with his insight, I asked him to see how this nonjudgmental *sitting in what is* could also be applied to his feelings of exhaustion and uselessness.

"Let's try it right now in session together. Let's just sit in this profound feeling and place of exhaustion together with no judgment."

So, that is what we did. For the next few minutes, we both just sat together in this total pervasive feeling of exhaustion, all with no judgment. And as we sat there for a few minutes, I could see and feel something was happening with Brad.

"What is going on?" I said.

"My God," he said. "This feeling of exhaustion has expanded and turned into a vast ocean."

I looked at him through the screen. "Very nice, Brad. What you thought was exhaustion is just the vast energy of the absolute. What is ashes is your own personal will, but that is okay as it was a mirage anyways. Now you can open up to do the will of the absolute, and can you see how much energy the absolute has?"

He looked back at me. "Infinite energy," he said with an abyss of madness look in his eyes.

"So Brad," I said, "can you see the cosmic hilariousness that what you thought was awful, your exhaustion, was just a doorway, your own awakening to the absolute and infinite energy."

Brad smiled serenely. "Yes I get it."

With that, we debriefed for a few more minutes and wound up our session and our work together. From loneliness and exhaustion, Brad had made the journey to a celebratory aloneness and feeling the vast energy of the absolute. All just by giving up waiting for some other wonderful experience, and just sitting in what is. The answer was already within his own experience.

We see that, at the end of the line, an acceptance of the fact that there is no way out is called for. There is no way to escape. By accepting that there is no sanctuary to seek, no experience to grab and escape into, by accepting our aloneness and exhaustion, we can rest at ease with existence itself. We no longer have to keep "waiting for Godot" as we see that endlessly waiting for something to happen, some wondrous experience, keeps us grasping at an elusive other, and this keeps us from recognizing that the mysterious awakening that we long have been looking for is right within our current experience itself. It is truly what Tony Parsons calls "an open secret" as it is all right here, right now, within whatever experience we are dealing with.[2]

PART FOUR

The Black Realm of Terror: Fear and Trauma

I often use the following analogy: non-dual awakening so energizes the whole system of awareness that any little root of emotional-psychological issue that remains on the cliff of the self—from which the jump into non-dual awareness takes place—suddenly magnifies into a huge tree of unresolved issues. Fear and trauma are notorious issues. If a person has not radically worked through fear and trauma and come to a place of understanding before non-dual awakening, then after awakening with the energy of the awesome abyss of existence, these issues will now be cataclysmic, a huge storm, a tsunami wave in the cosmic ocean. The terrorizing fear and trauma can become so chaotic and unmanageable that a person can feel as though they are suffering a perpetual panic attack.

Eventually we may see that these cut off, disowned aspects of being that have not been totally worked through are our powerful invitations for transformation. The intensity and discomfort of these holes cannot be denied. They show up in such an unmanageable and raw way, that it forces us to take a closer look at them. We have tried running away from them, regressing them, denying them, coping with them, picking ourselves up by our bootstraps against them, but in the awakening process, the absolute energy of existence has free rein and blows through them. Thus, over the next few chapters, we dive into issues of fear and trauma and see how these issues can be handled by non-dual awareness bringing a deepening of our non-dual awakening.

CHAPTER 14
Managing Fear Reinforces Fear

This took place during a non-dual group session.

"I need to go next," Kerry screamed. "I can't stand it anymore."

I looked over at her. I could see that she was obviously in a state of terror. I could sense the energy of a panic attack take over her. I asked her what was happening.

"Oh my god the energy is so intense," she said. "I am going to die."

As I looked over at her, I could see her hyperventilating. She actually thought she was going to die right there in the group. I could see that she was fighting the energy, fighting the panic, and the more she fought it, the worse it got.

"Give up fighting the fear," I said, "and just accept the energy."

Kerry looked over at me like I was crazy, so I repeated myself.

"I'm serious, don't fight the fear, just be one with it."

Kerry decided to go with my instructions, and as she did, as she accepted the fear, I could see that, as she gave up the fight, the energy surged in her and then crested, and then almost instantaneously broke away, all within about fifteen seconds. Kerry was shocked.

"I'm okay," she said.

This little vignette about Kerry exemplifies what I have witnessed with hundreds of people I have worked with over the years.

Fighting and trying to conquer fear just sets a person into a terrible spiral. But it is something almost all of us do. I, like most people, was one of those ones that tried to manage and cope with fear. I had collected a number of strategies over time, from awareness of cognitive distortions, to deep breathing, to being in the now, even a surrender strategy. None of them ultimately worked. Even a non-dual strategy of letting go, of surrendering was still a subtle strategy as I was still *doing* something. Strategies tend to work for a time and then they don't. When they are new, they may work for a while as some new energy is introduced into the mind–body system, but as the mind–body system becomes accustomed they become just another useless strategy.

Over time, I came to realize my whole approach to working with fear was missing the target. I was busy trying to manage and cope with fear, but never actually looked into it. Then I began to look into fear. The first thing I acknowledged was that all my efforts actually had not worked. It reminded me of a taped discourse I heard from Adyashanti in which the topic was fear and he invited a questioner who was trying to cope with fear:

"Listen to the intelligence of your experience. You keep saying, I can't, I can't, I can't… Even your own experience is telling you there is nothing you can do about fear."[1]

Brilliant! Adyashanti is pointing to the awareness that there is nothing that the "I" can do to overcome fear. The "I" is trying very hard, but it is not working. For this apparent being, it became clear that the "I" was trying to manage fear and failure could be the only result.

So if we let in that "I can't" what does that mean. It means that, when fear comes up, we realize there is *nothing that I can do*. Any trying is just more effort of the ego anyways and creates a psychological split between the "I" and the experience of fear. Nothing can be done, as any *doing* is counter-productive, it is just more ego. This realization of the futility of doing something with fear dramatically changes our perspective.

If there is nothing I can do, I don't do anything, and when fear comes up, I do nothing, and I am just one with the fear in the moment. It is like what J. Krishnamurti talked about in dealing with fear:

> When you see that you are a part of fear, not separate from it—that you are fear—then you cannot do anything about it; then fear comes totally to an end.[2]

How does fear come to an end? I am aware of it, with no judgment, in that moment, I see it is just vast energy, then miraculously fear itself is transformed.

Gangaji has a nice way of laying out this paradox of fear. She says:

> When there is an openness to fear, where can it be found? What a strange creature fear is. It exists only when there is resistance to its existence! When you stop and open to what you have resisted throughout time, you will find that fear is not fear. Fear is energy. Fear is space. Fear is the Buddha. It is Christ's heart knocking at your door.[3]

Thus, the awakening is right within the fear, not through trying to escape it. So rather than trying to manage fear, if a person is just one with fear with no gap, it dissolves by itself into vast energy to function in the moment. It is the resistance to fear that perpetuates its existence.

What use is there in abiding in non-dual being for the most part, but bringing the "I" and the mind in through the back door to manage fear. I have learned give it all up, surrender wholeheartedly to fear. In this way fear is naturally befriended. I am reminded of an incident a couple of years ago. Lawrence had been involved with me for eight years of transpersonal non-dual groups and then rebelled about five years ago by becoming preoccupied with the evolution vs. creation debate and by joining the Richard Dawkins evolution bandwagon. To me, I accept both the science perspective and what I would call a consciousness perspective, so I felt that I was out of the debate. However, Lawrence assumed I was on the creation side, and dropped out of attending the group. I was fine with this, as people need to do what they need to do. So, when I got the phone call at my university office that he had died suddenly in the kitchen of the counselling agency while microwaving his lunch, I felt surprised and sad, and thought to myself, *Well I probably don't even have to go to his funeral as it is a two hour drive and I hadn't seen him in five years.* Needless to say I was shocked when, two hours later, his wife phoned me and asked me to give a eulogy at the funeral in four days as that request was in the instructions Lawrence had left. I laughed to myself; he had the last laugh after all. And, of course, I agreed to do the eulogy talk.

Putting the phone down that night, I felt fear arising. *What have I got myself into? Funerals are crazy affairs.* For a few seconds, I felt the mind just trying to manage the arising fear, and starting to strategize. But instead of grabbing the fear and running with it with a bunch of strategies, I understood that nothing could be done. With my acceptance that nothing could be done, I immediately felt the fear surge and break into a vast serene energy. This was Tuesday evening and nothing could be done now to manage the fear for the Saturday funeral. I could make a few notes on a pad of paper for topic areas for my talk but that was about it.

Over the next few days, it seemed very much like what J. Krishnamurti had said in one of his talks. Fear can be like just watching a snake in the room with you. Surrendering to fear is an ongoing process, and the mind can be tricky as suddenly it can start grabbing a strategy to manage fear—in this case, improve the impending talk. During the next few days, I would just simply notice the occasional grabbing onto fear in the moment with a management strategy and let it all go once again. And as I sat through the service on the Saturday with a few hundred people, the eulogy was last, so I just enjoyed all of the other talks. When it was time for my talk, there was just a surrendering to the moment once again, and a total enjoyment of letting the absolute come through as I saluted Lawrence with authenticity and humour as he was man of many adventures. People at the reception later told me they were delighted with my zest and at times dark-hearted honouring of Lawrence, but in truth I could not even remember what I said as it was all just a spontaneous embracement in the moment. It was like the absolute coming through had given the talk. I was just a hollow bamboo.

The Open Sky of Insecurity

There seems to be another layer to this embracement of fear that needs to be addressed. Osho called awakening "the open sky of insecurity."[4] This is an acceptance of the fact that there is no such thing as psychological security that we get locked into trying to set up. So what does this lack of security mean? J. Krishnamurti, in his over fifty years of lecturing around the world, kept pointing to that there was nothing you could do psychologically to make moments in the future secure.[5] He also showed how the mind tries to manage fear for the future and through this process mind becomes fear itself.

It goes like this. To deal with fear arising for a future event, the mind tries to make the future event appear secure through coming up with a bunch of coping strategies, all of which are counterproductive as they actually help spiral fear even more and produce a second level of fear, fearing fear itself. One, in effect, becomes fearful of experiencing fear, which really can overwhelm a person's functioning, put the person on edge and make the person feel totally chaotically out of control. But if one can actually accept that there is nothing that can be done psychologically to prepare yourself for that future moment, then relaxation can happen. If one is going to do a presentation, one might still need to prepare all the powerpoint slides, but one can simply let go of psychologically preparing. One accepts the insecurity of the situation.

This acceptance of the insecurity of a future moment means letting go of psychological preparations to manage fear in an attempt to be secure in the future, and in the moment of the actual situation, one lets go as well. Not only is there no way to make a future moment secure, it is recognized that nothing can be done to make this moment secure as well. This moment could be my death, so rather than fighting this moment, or trying to hang on, I see that nothing psychologically can be done, and I let go and totally embrace this moment. In a total let go, I celebrate this moment, and enjoy the sublime vastness of energy as fear is totally absorbed with no resistance into the intensity of this moment.

Now to totally awaken through fear, we need to let go of our need to survive, and we see in the next chapter, how we must be willing to meet the greatest of all fears head on, the fear of non-existence itself.

CHAPTER 15
The Mother of All Fears: The Fear of Non-existence

Having worked with many people over the years, I have always been astounded at the fact that a person can have been on a non-dual journey for many years with many "awakening" experiences and lots of experience in the flow of existence, and yet still report being terrorized by a fear of non-existence. In our guts, we feel our primal rudimentary need to survive as we face no-self and nonexistence. Becoming aware of our primal grasping at survival, we can experience abject terror in which the fear of no-self can be overwhelming. As rebel non-dual teacher-writer Jed McKenna described:

> Fear.
>
> Fear of the hollow core. Fear of the black hole within. Fear of non-being.
>
> Fear of no-self.
>
> The fear of no-self is the mother of all fears, the one upon which all others are based. No fear is so small

or petty that the fear of no-self isn't at its heart. All fear is ultimately fear of no-self.[1]

Jed succinctly summarizes this point on fear when he says to his student Sarah, "And what is enlightenment but a swan dive into the abyss of no-self?"

In our non-dual journey from here to here, sooner or later we all have to accept the invitation head on of taking the plunge into McKenna's swan dive into the abyss of no-self. As we open up our mind and heart, we begin to be increasingly aware of consciousness opening up in our bellies, and we begin to feel the vast abyss of existence and, along with that, the threat of the end to our survival through a perceived sense of self-annihilation. As we look with awareness into our bellies and see no firm sense of "I", we can become overwhelmed with fear of not existing in the moment and may find ourselves desperately thrashing and trying to grab onto some sense of self in the knot of our belly as we defend against the oceanic abyss of no-selfhood.

This is truly where the rubber hits the road. In my experience, it is only in sitting in the black energy space of non-existence without judgment that it can be seen there is no independent self, and at the same time there is a presence which reveals itself to be a brilliant translucent light. The darkness of emptiness and nothingness is revealed as a translucent brilliant energetic fullness.

The problem here, though, is that there is a gap. The zero point of negative nothingness, the vast darkness which feels like non-being, non-existence and absence must be experienced and embraced, for it is out of this that the brilliant light of existence reveals itself. This, however, involves a quantum leap, a letting go, a willingness to go into the darkest possible experience of existence, and sit there, with no escape in the vacuum of non-existence darkness itself. The problem is people stampede away from experiencing this gap, for it feels too awesome and threatening. It is the last place most people want to be. They hesitate, backup, and refuse to go into it; they try to escape and run for the hills. Thus, because they have not worked it through, the "terror bird" of non-existence keeps haunting them in their everyday lives. It is like the old adage: *Wherever you go, there you are.* Sadly, even if you escape and run, you carry the black hole of non-existence with you wherever you go.

So the only way through this mother of all fears is to sit in the black non-existence energy itself. This is tricky as this the ultimate fear itself, and we can take one step forward, and two steps back in facing it.

Linda was like that, unsure, cautious. Previously, in her early thirties, she had began some intense surrender work with me in which she had been able to surrender to the dark abyss.[2] However, she had not quite finished her work on being one with the abyss in day-to-day life before she got swept up with some other issues like work, getting into grad school, and a new romantic partner. She had not completely surrendered to the abyss in her own aloneness. Not surprisingly, here we were, five years later, and the terror was back in full intensity, opening up in her life all over the place.

In our session together, as she started describing her experience, I could feel the annihilating terror come across her being and fill up the room in the moment. She let out a frightening "oh boy" desperate plea. I got right into it with her as the terror was overwhelming for her, and it was obvious she was feeling like she was going crazy.

"I am here with you in the abyss," I said. "See if you can stop fighting the abyss, as the abyss is you. You are the abyss, so there is nothing you can do, give up trying to save yourself, and just rest in no judgment."

Linda looked over at me stunned. I could see that for a few moments she was still struggling and then energetically she seemed to give up the struggle. There seemed to be a whoosh release as she became one with the energy, and the energy seemed to quickly climax and then fall away. I let her just sit there for thirty seconds and enjoy her new found vast peace. Then, I asked her:

"How are you doing now?"

"Wonderful," she said. "It is so serene."

She had a beautiful smile on her face. By giving up the fight and being one with the abyss with no judgment, the energy had transformed from annihilating terror to serene vastness, all in a matter of a couple of minutes.

Linda was shocked that the transformation of her fear of non-existence could be that easy and that fast. But that is how true surrender works, it is sudden, instantaneous, as it is a vertical movement of acceptance rather than a lateral movement through time. Later, as she embraced this acceptance in aloneness at her own apartment, she sent me this poem about her having a dissolution experience all by herself in which she was able to let go into the void despite initially feeling intense fear. Here is the poem:

> Dark surrender
> Give up the ghost
> Extinguish the flame
> In faith there is darkness
> There is no game
> "I" can't understand
> Who "I'm" not
> "I" can't be at peace
> Unless "I" rot
> Eye looks inward
> Direct vision is lost
> Nothing to pick up
> "I" burn like flame to moth

Linda has stopped the struggle and lets herself go through the gap. She recognizes it is something that the "I" can't understand, it is beyond mind. She dissolves into awareness, consumed like a moth by a flame.

Some authors have described this movement through no-self and non-existence as walking through the valley of death. Non-dual teacher Katie Davis described her own passage through this void of nothingness as:

> This void of nothingness is our salvation, when we are willing to walk into "the valley of the shadow of death" to explore. The void is qualified as the absence of everything, so we meet collective darkness. This absence is the Eternal Life's open doorway. We meet the collective fears of isolation, abandonment, hopelessness, helplessness and death. The root of humanity's cumulative fear is the fear of this void. ... The witness descends into the valley of aloneness and the Love that the witness is releases all illusion. Every manifestation of collective pain becomes the witness and the pain cannot withstand the Love of the merger...One could say that the emptiness of the void turns inside out into overwhelming fullness, which embodies the Totality as "I am That" ... The Essence is undifferentiated *Awake Joy* with no point of reference whatsoever.[3]

So it is here, in the darkest void, that the light of consciousness, the awake joy, reveals itself.

CHAPTER 16
Trauma: Healing through Catharsis and Embodied Experiencing

Working with people on their non-dual journey over the years, I have been astonished how trauma shows up as the issue blocking a celebration of non-dual being in day-to-day life. As part of our Abiding in Non-dual Being research project here at the University of Lethbridge, we talked to forty different non-dual teachers from around the world and they echoed a similar pattern. Working through trauma came up as a significant issue all around the world for people moving into non-dual being.

What is going on with trauma? It is evident that trauma leave us with holes in our being, and the problem with this, as Almaas laid out, is "a hole refers to any part of you that has been lost, meaning any part of you that you have lost consciousness of."[1] A hole is ultimately a loss of essence. These aspects of our being are not lost forever, but we are cut off from them. As we will see, the essence of a trauma experience involves a person saying to themselves, "This is so terrible, I can't handle it." In that moment the person freezes and dissociates from the feelings and intensity of that experience, leaving a hole of disconnected energy deep inside. This hole of disconnected energy stays inside our selves over time. We repress, disconnect, cope, gloss over and use our will to block out our black disconnected holes of trauma. This explains why so often when someone has a powerful non-dual awakening experience they can seem to go sideways into panic as these black holes of trauma, which may have been cut off from awareness for so long, suddenly get energized by the non-dual awakening experience. If you have not worked on your trauma experiences before your non-dual awakening, you will be forced into it after awakening. Non-dual awakening can feel like suddenly being a nuclear reactor of energy, but with trauma holes, you are a nuclear reactor with leaks, a disastrous situation. A little trauma leak is huge trouble.

For me, trauma was something I knew I needed to figure out. Having come from a household of a physically abusive and terrorizing doctor father and a heartfelt alcoholic nurse mother who died early from brain cancer, I had a black hole of trauma inside me all wrapped up in the abuse, terror and hatred I felt towards my father who ran the family household with tired crabbiness, self-righteous energy and eruptions of white hot anger. My mom, even though she descended into booze, stayed heartfelt, so I ended up not being as scarred by her loss of functioning, the loss that comes with chronic addiction. It was my father's rage legacy that kept tripping me up, even in adult life. I could feel something was wrong with my energy every time I bumped up against a terrorizing hierarchical male in a position of authority.

When I first joined the university in the late 1990s as an assistant professor, there was a self-righteous administrator, an Irish scientist, who was in charge of academics. Seeing him, I would just get livid and descend into my hatred. I knew I was over-reacting to his stories about the need to "take down the enemy" and his dismissive Ivory Tower attitudes. My intense reactive agitation was a sign to me that I had some healing to do as he really did not have much to do with me on a daily basis. He was really my boss' boss. So, even though I already had done some trauma work in my life, I decided to re-enter the fray of trauma healing.

Primal Therapy, Catharsis, and Psychodrama

Decades earlier, I had already done some preliminary primal therapy work in first year law school, screaming and pounding the mats with my angst.[2] I had followed this up in earnest with some intense trauma work early in my graduate school training in psychology. I started going to gestalt-bioenergetics weekend intensives based on the work of Fritz Perls and Alexander Lowen.[3] Foremost on my mind was the physical abuse I had endured from my father. I attended these weekend workshops to dissolve the pain stored in my mind–body and was encouraged to undergo intense catharsis release sessions. I thrashed on the mats, pounded tennis racquets, and yelled out to my imaginary father how much I hated him for what he had done. I remember at the time that the bio-energetic therapist would squeeze around my jaw area which was extremely tense and shut down, and this would cause me really to howl and express my rage, and kick on the mats like a madman. It was almost like my whole throat chakra and accompanying voice had been stifled. I could feel myself reclaiming my voice one scream at a time.

I followed this up with my own form of catharsis therapy by going for runs in the woods, stopping in the forest, and unleashing primal screams. I enjoyed this immensely for a while, it was such a release. But, at some point, this catharsis started to become routine and predictable. I could not deny that I was caught in a cycle of catharsis and release, but my understanding was not deepening, nor was I moving to a place of clarity and wholeness around my trauma.

I decided to push this even further by going into psychodrama work in the middle of my masters program.[4] Here I re-created the whole dysfunctional family system with the heartfelt yet incompetent now drunk mother, the self-righteous boss father, the new young nurse step-mother trophy wife, the rebel older brother who was off going to concerts and smoking pot, and a frightened twin brother who was innocently playing with his goldfish. I created my own emotional justice by giving family members the authentic feedback I had always needed to give them. Much to my chagrin, though, this brought a sense of release for a day or two, but no lasting sense of healing. I carried on.

Somatic Experiencing

A few years later, now in a faculty positionand projecting rage towards the Irish senior administrator, I knew I had to unpack my trauma even further. I dove in with a therapist into Somatic Experiencing, based on the work of Peter Levine, to reclaim my physical self and release the pent up arousal energy of trauma by allowing the thwarted defensive responses to complete themselves.[5] One experience I worked on a lot was that of being wrestled out onto the sun deck of the family home on a spring evening in grade eight and being given a forced razor hair cut by a towering white hot angry father that left me devastated, humiliated, and shame filled. Gone that day were my nice long curly locks, replaced by a ragged prisoner's haircut of hair two inches long. My dad at the time said, "If you cry, I will cut twice as much off." I remember myself being frozen, stifled. I could not believe what was happening. I did not want to cry as my bellowing angry father would cut all my hair off if I did.

In my own counselling sessions, I went back through the whole haircut experience with my therapist, and this time I reclaimed my physical self and let my body shake with energy as I broke out of the deer-in-the-headlights paralysis that I had been in at the time. I waved my arms wildly and, bolting for the door, escaped and ran out of the house. Boom, just like that I had cut short the traumatic physical abuse from my father, and re-claimed my physical power. This intense discharge of energy assisted my mind–body to return to a normal state. I now had some justice. I was able to bolt. I had my physical resourcefulness back.

However, I was still mystified. There seemed to be something missing. The return to joyous functioning was still not totally available. Catharsis, psychodrama and somatic experiencing had been very good, yet wholeness was still elusive, some understanding and healing was still missing. We will turn to that in the next chapter.

CHAPTER 17
The Missing Ingredients: Choiceless Awareness and Accepting Death

I had submerged myself into eastern contemplative traditions and awakening teaching for years while working in a western transpersonal psychology counselling and psychotherapy paradigm, and then one day I realized I already had the answer. It harkened back to a point Peter Levine made: it is not so much the trauma itself, but how it is interpreted that creates the lasting impact.[1] This reminded me of some of the teachings from Zen. The words of Sosan reverberated inside me. Sosan had pointed to a new way of orienting oneself, letting go of the mind's discriminating stance by giving up all the mind's accompanying judgments. Sosan says, "The Great Way is not difficult for those who have no preferences."[2] All of these preferences and judgments are the disease of the mind. With trauma, I could see it was one judgment after another about how terrible it was. I laughed to myself. How did I miss this? Nowhere do we see our judgmental mind so much like we do with trauma. With this understanding, there was now clarity that the most painful aspect of my trauma was my stance against the experience. It was not the actual experience that was the painful problem, but my stance that "this is terrible." It was my judgment, my opinion about the event that kept me locked in it. If I let go of my judgments, and my commentary and opinions, I could move into acceptance of the experience itself.

Seeing the need to drop the judging, critical voice even with trauma was a tremendous realization. In describing the non-dual perspective, Balsekar referred to this dropping as the letting go of the "split-mind."[3] The complaining "me" voice is dropped so now there is experiencing without the complaining experiencer.

This emphasis on no judgment, no preference seemed very similar to what J. Krishnamurti spent his whole life talking about, and that is choiceless awareness. In the experience of total attention, without judgment, there is no fear, no trauma:

> Fear is never an actuality; it is either before or after the active present. When there is fear in the active present, is it fear? It is there and there is no escape from it, no evasion possible. There, at that actual moment, there is total attention at the moment of danger; physical or psychological. When there is complete attention there is no fear. But the actual fact of inattention breeds fear; fear arises when there is an avoidance of the fact, a flight; then the very escape itself is fear.[4]

Inattention through escaping into our judgments creates fear and trauma. So with total attention, choiceless awareness in this moment, there is no fear or trauma. One day when asked what his total secret was, Krishnamurti said, "I don't care what happens." His answer is the epitome of choiceless awareness, not caring, not judging what happens.

It seemed now it was clear I had to go back and revisit these old traumas with total attention and no judgment, no split-mind, just re-experience them fully.

Re-visiting Old Traumas

With this new found focus on choiceless awareness, I re-explored the significant traumas I had gone through in my life, the physical abuse from my dad, the drinking and the subsequent brain cancer death of my mother, and being fired from a couple of jobs. I was shocked to discover that by just recreating and re-witnessing these experiences with no judgment, no separate-self comment, something shifted. It was like I could watch these experiences and for the first time, experience them without a deep conflict and, with this, let them go. In this way, I now experienced the actual feelings of the situations, which I had never done before as I was so busy escaping them. I discovered that avoidance was far worse than the actual emotions. Terror, fear, abandonment, shame, horror can all be experienced with no judgment. The beauty, I discovered, is that all of these feelings are just energy, and when experienced without judgment just turn into spacious energy, and disperse naturally without effort. I did not have to hang onto these experiences by telling myself how horrible they were. I could let go.

It was also clear to me that this focus on no-judgment and choiceless awareness could become a central aspect of my emerging non-dual psychotherapy approach to trauma. I did however need a deepening of the no-self aspect as we see in the following section.

Trying to Survive No Matter What

As I worked through these traumas, I came to realize that there was a pervasive undercurrent to all of these traumatic experiences that I had not really fully acknowledged in my awareness. I needed to bring no-judgment, acceptance, and choiceless awareness to one of the greatest fears of all, death of the self. Put in another way, the lust for survival gets totally activated in life-threatening trauma situations. In our guts, we instinctually grasp at surviving no matter what. Thus, when we are in the middle of a trauma-provoking life-threatening experience, it puts us in total fear and panic as we are afraid we are going to not make it and are going to die. So, any threat to our survival, with our primal grasping at surviving, is interpreted as being terrible by the mind.

The way out of this perpetual seizing on surviving-no-matter-what orientation is to acknowledge that it is the nature of existence that life is dangerous and our survival is continually up for grabs in each moment. This moment might be the moment of our death. But we do not want to face this. And to me, as a non-dual therapist, it is almost a good sign when I hear a person is having panic attacks all the time, that means the fear of death and not surviving has now become transparent in being. We can only deal with something if it is in our awareness; it is impossible if it is repressed, frozen or hidden in our unconscious.

So, in trauma our psychological and physical safety of the self gets threatened. We don't want to die; we want to survive no matter what. As we work on our trauma, we can become aware of the primal grasping at survival. With an instinctual arm thrusting out from our bellies, we grasp at surviving at all costs. And with trauma, our lust for survival may even mean we need to disassociate to a safe place when the experience itself is too overwhelming.

Overall, we see that, in a life and death traumatic experience, we can become overwhelmed with the fear of not existing and desperately grab onto some sense of self in the knot of our belly as we defend against the oceanic abyss of potential self-annihilation. We can see then that deeply embedded in trauma is the fear of death and no-self. And if true healing is going to take place, this fear of death and no-self that emerges within trauma must be resolved.

In my own journey, I could see that I would always be in a state of trauma if I did not surrender to the threat of death. If I was always trying to survive at all costs, I would always be in fear of "what is", as the threat of death to the self is always present. In short, I would always be caught in the grips of trauma and fear. I would always be in a fear-based existence. I did not want to live perpetually in fear so I explored further.

The Second Missing Ingredient: Dying to Self, the Great Death

In my own journey, grasping at the self, which showed up in trauma, was also related to seeking non-dual awakening. While I had been on a long quest into contemplative and non-dual traditions, there was still a separate self who had not died, seeking awakening. Ironically, this was the same self that was trying to survive in trauma experiences. It was through dying to the seeker, that I was able to let go of hanging on to the self in the middle of trauma episodes.

My seeking had lost its luster and had become more of an experience of feeling intense misery, suffering, and absolute hopelessness. I had grown exhausted from my seeking. Turning to rot and absolute hopelessness, my seeking had been a total failure. As I mentioned in an early chapter of the book, one day, a total out-of-control experience of exhaustion swept over me, and a hopeless feeling that I would not be able to do one more thing overtook me. I just accepted the invitation to relaxedly drop into utter effortlessness and drowning. It was literally like falling to the ground. So, I surrendered. I went down quietly, without splashing around, and just allowed myself to be drowned totally into existence. This was the death of my total mind–body project, "the Gary awakening project." Things were over, and I sat calmly in this place where I was no more. I relished the painless joy of no effort and the revealing translucent light of existence.

This acceptance of death of self immediately helped with my trauma. I could now work through trauma to a deeper level, for I was not desperately grasping onto my separate self. I was now *a dead man walking* as the saying goes. Death is destiny as Lao Tzu pointed out.[5] We all are going to end in death. All paths lead to death. Knowing and accepting this now, frees our lives and changes the gestalt. I liked Osho's commentary on this poignant saying of Lao Tzu:

> Once you accept death many things are immediately accepted. In fact if you accept death as part of life, then all other enemies are also accepted as part of friendship because the basic duality dissolves, the duality of life and death, being and non-being. If the basic duality is resolved, then all other dualities are just superficial, they dissolve. Suddenly you are at home – eyes are clear, no smoke is in them, and perception is absolutely clear, no darkness is around.[6]

With death accepted, trauma is no longer the enemy. I could accept these events, for I was no longer desperate to survive. I was already free. There was no person, just the vastness of existence. I did not need to go anywhere or grab onto anything for support. I could now just relax into awareness of this and enjoy the play of existence in this moment. I was free.

Now, I could see through the illusion of trauma. There is no separate self to hang onto, but because we believe in the illusion of self, we hang on for dear life. Seeing we are already dead and that there is no separate self brings instant freedom even in the face of apparent trauma. And seeing this is instantaneous. This realization can be astounding. Pivotal is to see, in the absolute intensity of this moment, that there is no self. There is no person here and there never has been. There is not a self to be traumatized or to die. Nobody is here to be traumatized. This full emptiness becomes all of existence. Only the whole is, and the reality of death is accepted in the moment. There is a movement beyond death. In choiceless awareness, existence itself is embraced and there is no independent separate self to hang onto.

The Art of Dying: Being Ready to Die in Each Moment

The key link back to healing trauma, then, is the understanding that the apparent individual needs to have already accepted death. Life and death is fully embraced in each moment without grabbing the separate self and the need for perpetual survival. I willingly embrace death in each moment. As Osho laid out in The Art of Dying:

> Never possess anything—and then you are ready to die. Possessiveness is the problem, not life itself. The more you possess, the more you are afraid to lose. If you don't possess anything, if your purity, if your spirit is uncontaminated by anything, if you are simply there alone, you can disappear any moment; whenever death knocks on the door it will find you ready. You are not losing anything. By going with death you are not a loser. You may be moving into a new experience.[7]

The problem is, if we lose our non-dual awareness, we start grabbing back onto the separate self and the props that maintain it such as relationships, jobs, wealth, spiritual experiences, all the things the ego grabs onto, and with that accumulation comes fear. We don't want to die! If we don't accumulate, we can accept this could be the moment of our death, and be in the vast empty sky of existence. We stay in choiceless awareness and can be trauma free.

The key is accepting the reality of death in each moment. This intense understanding let the appearance known as Gary be released from the vice grip of trauma.

With this awareness, I found that new experiences that were previously potentially traumatizing no longer traumatized me. Nothing terrorized me, for I had let go of my need to survive. Meeting a bear on my run in the woods, being forced by another vehicle over a cliff while driving, were met with the recognition and acceptance that this could be the moment of death. With this acceptance, there was just serene stillness in the moment, and whatever happened, happened. The bear left me alone, the SUV crashed into a tree and was totalled, and we all walked away unscathed.

In the next two chapters, we will look at how I applied this new emerging non-dual approach to trauma work with clients in working with early childhood abandonment trauma and then in one of the most intense areas of all, sexual abuse.

CHAPTER 18
Healing Childhood Abandonment

Clients on a non-dual journey contact me as they feel stuck in their journey right now. Often, they are having issues around relationships and an inability to be alone. Working on the issue, we discover that they have been fighting a feeling of abandonment since childhood. They have been rejecting an experience of being abandoned as a young child, and being left alone with no support. To avoid the pain of this "terrible" experience, at the time they unconsciously froze and disassociated from the pain, as it was felt too much to handle. As a result, since then they have been carrying this deep pain of abandonment in their guts, and are perpetually striving to make relationship connections to avoid feeling the pain. But, wherever they go the pain is still with them.

Scott's Nice Guy Persona Covers His Abandonment

Scott was smiling on the outside, but deep down he was a person frozen in a limbo state. He had been abandoned as a child, and carried the dreaded abandonment feeling ever since. When he was seven, his parents split up, and suddenly he was put into foster care. He had carried on after that, and now forty years later, as a family counsellor and gambling specialist, he had come to terms with the fact that something had felt off for a very long time. He had been a nice guy covering up his feeling of deficiency for so long, he needed to address it as he had never been able to enjoy his life. In our session together, Scott told me that he had been a nice guy for so long, taking care of everybody else's needs, that it had just become a habit even though it felt totally fake as that is not how he felt deep inside.

When I asked him about how this pattern started, Scott sighed:

"It started in my childhood. I can remember as a young boy, being seven, and feeling totally frightened as my dad was chasing me around the house. I ended up hiding in a kitchen cupboard, and I could hear him bellowing out for me, and I sat there cowering, feeling very frightened. In that moment, I felt abandoned in life as it felt like there was nobody to take care of me. Right after that incident, my parents broke up, and I was put into foster care for a year."

"How did that abandonment feel?" I said.

Scott sighed. "It felt like I was a little boy on a beach, down by the ocean side, and I was there by myself with nobody around anywhere, and it was very frightening."

I paused for a second. "Have you ever been back on that beach?"

Scott shook his head.

"Why don't we go there now?" I said. Scott nodded his head, so I proceeded.

"Imagine you are the seven-year-old little boy, and you are on the beach today, all by yourself. Just close your eyes and see yourself down on the beach."

I let Scott take the time to set up the visualization in his head. "Are you there now?" I said.

Scott nodded his head.

"How are you feeling?"

Scott took a moment. "Awful, I feel all alone, and frightened, I don't know why this is happening to me."

I pressed on. "Now Scott, as you are sitting there, I want you to say to yourself no judgment. You are just going to be in the feelings of abandonment, and fear, and awfulness, without judgment. Can you do that now?"

I could see Scott try to settle into it. I made it easier for him by having him focus on one feeling:

"To make it easy for you, how about just sitting in the abandonment feeling. You are on the beach, and all abandoned. Just sit with that with no judgment."

Scott sat there, and after a few minutes I could see his energy shifting.

"What is going on?" I said.

"It is funny, the abandonment feeling use to feel like a tight dark ball of energy in my stomach, but it is expanding."

"Good," I said. "Keep that up, be one with it with no judgment."

I let Scott just sit there, eyes closed, one with his abandonment. He sat there for a few more minutes.

"What is going on now?" I asked.

"It is expanding and now it is not just in my belly, but it is now becoming bigger, taking up my whole body, even it feels outside my body. And now it feels much lighter, just like a sublime aloneness."

"Stay with that," I urged.

I let Scott stay there until I saw, with a flicker of his closed eyes, him starting to pull up into his head.

"You just got into your head," I said. "What happened?"

"I started thinking about how I am going to keep this wonderful feeling of serene spaciousness."

"You got back into your mind again, Scott. All you need to do is remind yourself no judgment, and then be back with the experience once again. For homework, you can sit in this abandonment for a few minutes every night, all with no judgment. The key thing here is that you have been carrying this feeling of abandonment in your guts your whole life, always running away from it, and trying to make connections with others, so you did not have to feel it, but everywhere you went, the abandonment feeling was there. So being a nice guy did not work out for you because you still had the feeling of abandonment in your guts. But here today, as you sat in your abandonment, you came to realize that it is actually just spacious aloneness if it is accepted. So now you can realize that even your seven-year-old self was okay, you just did not realize it at the time. And now you are okay with the abandonment feeling, it just your vast aloneness. You do not need to chase relationships to be okay. You now can now set boundaries because you are okay with your own fundamental aloneness. I think that is pretty good work for one day."

Scott smiled. "Thank you, Gary."

This is actually a very common occurrence: feeling devastating abandonment as a child in which parents or other caregivers left the child alone at too young an age, resulting in the child being overwhelmed by loneliness and feeling abandoned in an alien world. I have had clients talk about being left to weed the garden at three, or having parents out partying and leaving them alone at night in grade one, or watching an intense drunken screaming match between parents at seven, and feeling totally abandoned, huddled in bed. This abandonment feeling can be a profound transformational invitation for the person who wants to change a pattern of a being caught in compulsive "nice person" codependency and heal the dark hole of abandonment directly.

CHAPTER 19

The Deep Wound: A Non-dual Approach to Sexual Abuse Healing

So many of the trauma experiences clients bring to work on in non-dual therapy are not physical near death experiences per se, but those of intense sexual abuse usually from childhood. Because of the intensity of the energy wrapped up in these experiences and the total threat to the body–mind system, I have had to be mindful of the clinical notion of safety for the client which needs to be embraced but eventually transcended.[1] The key has been for me to work within what Ogden, Minton, & Pain have called the client's window of tolerance for optimal processing in which the client is not in a state of hyper-arousal with a flood of sensations, intrusive imagery, extreme emotional reactivity, disorganized processing, and hyper-vigilance, nor is the client in a state of hypo-arousal with an absence of sensation, numbing of emotions, disabled cognitive processing, and reduced physical movement. Too hyped up, or too numbed down does not work. What is needed is the middle zone.[2]

To work in the optimal window of tolerance zone for trauma, preliminary work can be done in sessions before focusing specifically on the trauma. This preparation can stretch to a number of sessions depending on the client's background in the non-dual approach. We initially work on the basics of non-dual awareness, such as total awareness in the moment, inquiring into the self-contraction, processing dark emotions with no judgment, dropping from the head into the belly through understanding that the mind does not have the answer, letting go of our stories, and resting in presence. This preliminary work prepares the ground for non-dual trauma work and helps the client be in the window of tolerance zone for trauma work. I have also found that many of these clients have already done extensive healing and therapy work on their trauma with more conventional therapy approaches but have not come to a full healing yet, hence they want to work on their trauma from a non-dual perspective.

When proceeding to trauma work with a client in session, the emphasis is to return to fully and non-judgmentally embrace the traumatic experience, letting the energy, emotions and physical body have its free rein and expression. This work goes beyond somatic experiencing in that the non-judgment stance takes us straight to ego death and letting go of the separate self contraction so the client can drop the split-mind, the grasping at surviving, and then rest in being and essence. Ironically, our worst experiences can be have the most transformational potential, for working through the agonies of trauma can be an awakening experience into no-self awareness and non-dual being as we find stillness and essence within the trauma experience itself.

When we extend non-dual trauma work into sexual abuse, we have to even have more clarity about the power of non-judgmental choiceless awareness as the layers of stories, feelings, judgments, societal and counselling stories can be very thick. Often, when working with a client who has worked on childhood sexual abuse in therapy for many years, we find that the client has never returned fully to the actual experience itself as it was seen as too frightening. That judgment must be unpacked. Non-dual healing happens within the centre of the trauma experience itself, and so the client must learn to meet the pain of the experience head on, with no judgment.

In the following example, the client who had previously been in a more traditional form of counselling for a couple of years learns to sit in the actual experience of the sexual abuse for the first time, and reclaim the emotions she never actually felt in the first place when disassociated from the terrible feelings. But first, here are some words of caution for therapists.

A Note for Therapists

As we proceed with this case study, it must be noted that a non-dual approach will only work if you have worked through your own trauma with no-judgment choiceless awareness as well as having surrendered to death so you have seen non-dual awakening right within your own trauma experience. This implies you are free to sit with a client with any experience that is brought forward, no matter how apparently gruesome it might seem to the mind, as it is seen it is all workable. The non-dual therapist needs to have clarity about this. I have had referrals from therapists who attempted to utilize a non-dual approach to trauma but abandoned it mid-stream with their client as they themselves became confused. This is unfortunate as it encourages a client to collapse and seize even more on the trauma experience. Furthermore, the therapist can have counter-transference issues in which his or her own personal trauma is set off or the therapist can become vicariously traumatized working with the client's trauma. Clarity here for the therapist is essential.

Therapists need to be leery of falling into sympathy, which beginning therapists get lost in as they take the trauma of a client on as their own, and set off their own lifetime of trauma issues (counter-transference). This is a kind of a co-dependency in which therapists lose their own awareness and take on the client's experience as their own. A simple way of saying this is to say that beginning therapists can get lost in the belly of the client. Now there are two people going down in flames rather than one. Rather than being lost in the trauma with the client, a therapist needs to be both empathic, which is to say understanding and communicating back to the client what the client is or has experienced with all its levels, and empowering, which is very important in trauma work so that clients learn how to be free themselves. Overall, instead of sympathy, my sense is what is called for is a therapist with loving open-hearted receptivity, who is empathic, non-judgemental, knows that all these experiences potentially happen to us all, and recognizes the awakening potential of the client. As the therapist becomes more mirror-like and clear, it seems that the ability to accurately perceive what the client has gone through intensifies, as well as the capacity to provide pointers and invitations for freedom.

On the other side, therapists need to be mindful to not set themselves up as superior when working with clients. The non-dual therapist has had to look intimately at trauma and has seen the non-dual perfection right inside the experience of trauma itself but knows life goes on and on—and who knows what is around the corner? We are all apparent beings on this journey of awakening in which there is no final stop point, as on and on it goes. In addition, as non-dual awakening is situated right inside trauma itself, it means non-dual awakening is accessible to all, some people just have not realized it yet. Airs of superiority and hierarchy hide the fact that only nobodies are awakened. I have seen non-dual therapists and teachers come from a place of superiority and hierarchy and months or years later a huge catastrophe hits, often with some significant shadow issues of one sort or another. Authenticity means recognizing each of us can only live one moment at a time, and can not guarantee the next moment. It also means that life can throw a curveball that we did not see coming, so we need to be careful about our grand proclamations of having it all figured out forever.

I also use to think that, as a male therapist, I needed to stay completely away from working with females on their sexual abuse experiences. However, over time females have began to ask me to work with them on their sexual abuse. The feedback I received is that they appreciated that I could meet with them in being and embrace non-judgment so that, together, we could work at untangling all of the levels of stories and judgments. In this way, they could free themselves to reclaim their feelings in a non-judgmental way, access their physicality, and find themselves reclaiming their essence naturally which they thought they had lost. In this work, I come from a place of openness, being to being. The client may come from a place of gender or sexualized being, but the invitation is made to drop into being. In any event, freedom lies beyond gender, beyond sexual identity, beyond trauma when non-dual being is opened up to that which has always been here.

We will now turn to look at the healing Myrna went through in working through an intense childhood sexual abuse experience utilizing a non-dual approach.

Watching the Blood Going Down the Drain

It all came tumbling out. Myrna explained how, when she was seven, she was caught with her friend in the bathroom with her friend's dad. She slowly recounted the experience. Time seemed to slow down to an eternity. For hours she and her friend were sexually abused by her friend's father, and in horror she kept getting this image of watching the blood go down the bathtub drain. Now, as Myrna was sharing the story, she was hyperventilating and wanting to escape, bolt from the bathroom and the therapy room. She looked over at me and said:

"This is too awful, I can't face this. I do not know what to do."

I paused, and looked at her straight in the eye. "You have described what has happened. Now view the situation without judgment, let go of all your opinions as to what is happening, just be with it."

She looked back at me frightened. "Okay."

I looked across at her and could see her whole body just shaking in intensity. "No judgment, Myrna, just accept whatever arises."

I knew that Myrna, in her previous trauma work with other therapists, had gone only to a certain level, talking about the experience. She needed to go deeply into the experience itself for true healing, and discover her essence. Here was her chance.

Peter Levine recognized that the trapped and heightened energy of traumatic experience needs to be discharged from the body. He instructed, "Resolve arousal states by promoting discharge of the vast survival energy mobilized for life preserving action."[3] Myrna was shaking in the moment, and I asked her to do nothing about the shaking, have no judgment, and just let it run its course. Her energy and shaking seemed to really intensify over the next couple of minutes, and I reminded her to stay with it with no judgment. After a few minutes her shaking and intensity seemed to crest like a wave and then fall. All of a sudden she sat there very still and calm like.

"What is happening?" I said.

"I felt the terror very intensely," she said. "But I stayed in no judgment, and it just broke. Now I just feel calm and serene. Everything is okay."

There seemed to be something more than a restoration of what Levine called "self-regulation and dynamic equilibrium" in which "you have a secure home base within your organism."[4]

I asked her what it was.

She said, "I feel the underlying essence."

I smiled. "You thought you lost who you were, but you just re-discovered it was with you all the way along. Beautiful."

So now, in healing her trauma, Myrna miraculously found a deeper experience of who she was. She re-acquainted herself with her underlying essence. Her psychic content of trauma had made her feel heavy and dark, but now with choiceless awareness, she felt her underlying being as essence as Almaas had described, "a luminous night sky, transparent and pure."[5] Put it another way, Myrna had discovered her being underneath the apparent trauma.

When I asked what she understood to be the key to her healing, she replied, "No judgment." She also said she really appreciated how, when she looked at me straight in the eyes as she described her trauma and the torment she went through, she saw calmness, openness and no judgment. This helped her feel support as the connection to another being in essence brought her courage in re-experiencing of the trauma. She could then face what she had desperately avoided for so long—the terror. And miraculously she found out that it was not the terror itself that was so hard, it was all her judgments and attempts to avoiding facing it. Being one with it, the terror dispersed into energy all by itself. In describing the healing Myrna went through, it seems very fast, but that was the case. The intense healing took place in fifteen minutes.

When we had a wrap-up session later in a couple of weeks, Myrna reported that she had remained in her essence for a number of days afterwards, and a new place of healing had emerged. My sense is that she had done a lot of preliminary work earlier around her trauma, developed a window of tolerance, but never had actually stood within her experience with no judgment, thus she never had found release and freedom. Now, with this no-judgment work, she had gone through a major shift. This experience no longer defined her. Yet it was also evident that there was more to face. To extend her healing, she needed to work through her stance and resistance to death. She was always grasping at her need to survive in the moment. I left her with the challenge over the next few months to give up her grasping for survival and to accept death in each moment, and to relax into her non-dual being. Our work together stopped, as we had agreed to a few intense emergency sessions to work on her trauma, but she was planning on returning to work with her usual therapist that she had seen for the last three years.

Myrna and Her Bible Camp Counsellor

I was surprised when, a few months later, Myrna phoned me to set up some more trauma work. I had thought we had worked on the central piece. When we met, Myrna explained to me she was now ready to deal with an experience she had always avoided sharing, she had never talked about it with her previous therapists. I encouraged her to go on. She explained when she was twelve she had gone to a summer Christian Bible Camp for a week. She was rebellious and had lots of energy and did not necessarily go along with the rules of the camp. One day, one of the female camp counsellors, a woman about twenty-five asked to see her in one of the counsellor cabins. Myrna had thought this was odd but went to see the woman anyways. When she got to the door, the counsellor told her to come in and sit down on the bed. The counsellor went over to the door and locked it and dead-bolted it. With this, Myrna's alarm bells started to ring internally.

Here, Myrna stopped recounting the story, and looked over at me, eyeing me for any sign of judgment. I told her take your time.

"I might as well just dive in," she said. "The counsellor told me that I had been bad and evil and needed to be taught a lesson, and healed. I was dumbstruck. She stripped me of my clothes while I lay on the bed paralyzed in shock. She tied my legs and arms to the bed. Then, she spread wine over all of my body and rubbed it into my skin. I was mortified and felt nausea. After a few minutes which seemed like hours, she said to me we need to get you cleaned up, and took me over to the shower and washed me."

With that, Myrna stopped her story and looked over at me.

"This is huge," I said, "with lots of layers. Now, just sit in this experience with no judgment, and just feel what it was like. Just allow feelings to be there without judgment."

As Myrna got in touch with her feelings, all with no judgment, I sat there right with her in the experience. I allowed the pain of the experience to be present to me. Myrna described her shock, not knowing what was going on, her shame as she was told by the counsellor that she was bad, and needed healing, and the nausea as the counsellor poured the wine all over her body. Then she described the sense of betrayal she was feeling, and then more shame as the counsellor told her she needed to have a shower to get all cleaned up. Even though she knew she was the victim, she felt like a sinner.

I supported Myrna to stay with these emotions with no judgment, and feel the intensity of them. After a while a flash of energy went through Myrna, and I asked her what was going on. She said she felt rage. I said just go with that.

"What do you want to say to this woman," I said, "this so-called camp counsellor?"

I pointed to an empty chair.

"She is right here, tell her how you are feeling."

Myrna tore right into her. "Fuck you, you fucking bitch for what you did to me… you took my innocence away, fuck you."

Myrna was very energized, and I could tell that there was more where this came from.

"Tell her how much you hate her," I said.

With no hesitation, Myrna screamed, "I hate your guts, you fucking bitch. I hate you. I wish you would go and die somewhere. I hate you for what you did to me. Fuck you…"

"That seems almost complete," I said. "Is there anything else?"

"I am going to have to lay a beating on you, you bitch, because you deserve it."

I looked over at Myrna and could see her readiness to beat this counsellor up. She was reclaiming her physical self that had been paralyzed in the moment. We stopped our catharsis empty chair processing at that, and began to debrief the session.

Myrna reported feeling relieved and much lighter but also very exhausted which is always a good sign for deep processing work. We planned for her to follow up and check in with me in a day. We debriefed the session for a few more minutes and then we left it at that for the day.

When Myrna came back the following day, she had a smirky grin on her face. I asked her what was going on. She reported she had stayed up almost all night and enjoyed the imagery of laying a beating on this woman. She really enjoyed herself. Through this, she had taken her own power back and felt liberated. I never condone any actual physical contact between victim and perpetrator, but it can be important for the victim to release anger, hurt and hatred at an empty chair, a pillow, a tree out in the woods, or an imaginary role play.

After a few minutes of letting her enjoy the sweetness of revenge, I asked her:

"Were you in any way responsible for what happened to you?"

"No," she said right off the bat, as that is what she always had said.

"Slow it down, are you responsible for this in *any* way?"

She sighed to herself. She recognized she already, the day before, had revealed herself.

"Yes I remember," she said, "I had a weird feeling, when the counsellor told me to meet her up in the cabin, that something very strange was up, and I just ignored the feeling."

"Ah" I said, "so you have your own two percent part, very small but also a part, you were not a total victim, as you ignored your gut telling you something is wrong."

Myrna looked over at me. "Yes that's true. I felt the weirdness, but I did not pay attention to it."

"So," I said. "Can you see how, by avoiding what your gut was saying to you, you betrayed yourself?"

Myrna laughed to herself.

"Totally, and I have not wanted to take responsibility for this piece at all."

With this, something seemed to click with Myrna, a completion was taking place. Owning her two percent had been a missing piece.

I invited Myrna to sit there, and process how it felt.

"My god," she said. "The trauma is dissolving all by itself, the whole story is disappearing."

"Yes," I said. "By letting go of your splits and judgments and staying in the experience it dissolves by itself. And the final piece in the puzzle is taking your small part of responsibility for what happened, your two percent, and now the whole trauma, the whole story is dissolving by itself. You do not have to define yourself by this trauma anymore."

Myrna smiled.

We spent a few more minutes winding up the session that day, and Myrna did not need another session on her trauma; tremendous healing had happened. Through embracing choiceless awareness, feeling all the feelings with no judgment, and watching them become spacious, and by embracing her physical self, in this case imaging laying a beating on her perpetrator, and by finally owning up to her small part in all of it, Myrna was able to move into essence, and the trauma story dissolved by itself. It was wonderful healing for her, for now she did not have to secretly live with this trauma anymore.

This was a complex non-dual healing, for there had been so many levels of judgments attached to the story: judgments about the same sex aspect of the abuse, judgment about being a bad person who needed spiritual healing, screwed up judgments projected upon her from the perpetrator who pretended to be acting from a good and spiritual place helping cleanse the client's badness, lots of levels of judgments to let go of. And now Myrna felt free. We also see that Myrna felt empowered to take her healing into her own hands. She acted out an imaginary physical retaliation against her perpetrator, which she wished she had been capable at the time when she was twelve, but was paralyzed. But now she is accessing her previously frozen physical resources. As well, she now has empowered herself to be trauma resilient through her embracement of no-judgment and her freed up physicality—all a remarkable shift for Myrna.

PART FIVE

Veiled Darkness: Diving into the Deep Dark Realms

In a person's transformational journey it may seem that everything under the sun has been worked through yet a disconnected darkness persists. In my own experience, and working with non-dual clients, this may be an invitation to check out realms stored in the person's deep unconscious. It is not important to hold a belief that these realms even exist. Rather, when a person intentionally openly accesses realms such as past life memories, birth trauma or even hell realm experiences, the process can result in liberation as dark holes are brought into awareness and constricted energy is released. The proof is in the transformation. Bringing the light of awareness to our deepest, darkest realms can sometimes be the long lost key that allows us to naturally surrender into non-dual awareness without the energy being hijacked through a dark hole in our being. We explore these darkest realms and the invitation for transformation that they provide through the next chapters.

CHAPTER 20
Past Life Trauma: Finding the Missing Key

Sometimes people are mystified. They do intense amounts of self-growth and trauma work on all of their issues and still something feels wrong. If a person has tried everything, and is still not free, it makes sense to check into the possibility of past life issues. Psychiatrist, Brian Weiss, discovered the importance of past life issues when using hypnotherapy with a patient who had not been able to unglue the source of her issues. This client spontaneously regressed into the time period of a past life and identified the source of the anxiety issues that were haunting her in her current life. Working through the issues in this regression session led to a complete and immediate cessation of her symptoms.[1]

In my own life, early in my meditation practice, it seemed like some very intense past life experiences crashed through me. I remember, only a couple of years into intense meditation, having an experience of all of existence turning into white light and kind of a flowers showered experience. What was weird about the whole thing is it kind of crashed over me like a whole piece, like a big chunk of life. I did not know what to think of it at the time, for it was very intense and beyond my level of understanding. More troubling though was the re-experiencing of a sense of tremendous torture, and being locked away as a prisoner. I did not know where this came from. Not knowing how to handle it at the time, I put it away.

Unfortunately, what a person represses or denies, and stores in unconsciousness will still come back to haunt him or her. I had already experienced lots of trauma healing, yet occasionally there was a piece of something that I would feel. Once every few of years I would get a sense of impending jail and black doom, and I could not identify where it came from. As I wanted a full embracement of abiding in non-dual being, I decided purposely to embrace some past life therapy to see if it would help to find the source of this experience and sort it out.

I was not wrapped into the official debate about the reality of past lives. To me something of past lives had shown up in my consciousness. I did not care if it was an actual past life that I could prove, or simply part of what Jung called the collective unconscious,[2] or what Stan Grof and all of his work in holotropic therapy revealed about the whole history of the human race and planetary and cosmological consciousness.[3] To me, it did not matter because somehow I was still caught. Something in my consciousness was haunting me.

I did some work with a past life regression therapist, and the whole experience quickly exploded within me. It was very similar to the experience of torture that had exploded upon me in my early twenties. In the session I was regressed directly to a prison camp. In this vision I, as a young man, had languished for a while with a feeling of being in hell, and then one day the order was given for me to be executed. As I was led away, I felt how extremely horrific it was to feel my young life, with so much promise, being snuffed out. I felt totally betrayed by existence.

Unlike what I had heard about past life therapy in which awareness of the experience was enough, I did not feel healed. So, I decided to work on this experience with a very heartfelt transpersonal psychotherapist whom I trusted very much. We went back to my shocking execution and visited the horror of the pain and the evil. This time however, I did things differently. I said to myself, *This is the moment of my death, I accept.* What was remarkable is that things changed instantly for me. I did not even feel any physical pain, for in a serene way I was out of my body, watching my body crumple. I felt compassion for this life ending so abruptly, but it was serene, and I was not grabbing into the "I" in any way. I surrendered. So much serene stillness and calmness and love were now felt in the re-experienced time of being executed.

This deep healing opened up by embracing choiceless awareness and accepting my death. I saw that it had been a traumatic death, but now, with no judgment and accepting the moment, as the moment of my death, it was now okay, even a beautiful transformation into light. The total darkness in the valley of death had turned into a translucent light. I had not lost the essence of who I was. What a beautiful gift, accepting death in the moment, even an execution. It was okay, it was a gift to let go into vastness, the eternal absolute, all with no judgment.

The true test of intense past life work is the impact on one's current life. I immediately felt the difference. I no longer felt that occasional black hole prison feeling. And now having accepting my own death with love, this freed my "killer" archetype to merge with love. Love and the "killer" were no longer split within my consciousness, they were intermingled together in the sacredness of the moment.

A Non-dual Explanation of Past Lives

People often ask what does a focus on past lives have to do with the non-dual penetrating insight that everything is contained in this moment? In fact, the paradox is that it is all about existence in the here and now; all of life, past, present and future is contained here in the beyond time eternity of this moment.

In this moment it is seen that there is no actual separate self "I" existence, so what is all of this talk about past lives then? It is like there is no continuity of self that continues, but our illusions and our mind can carry on. Like Adi Da always said, "Before you die, you make the mind, after you die, the mind makes you."[4] So a person dies, and the thoughts and desires carry on glued together under the illusion of this solid sense of "me." It is easy to see this all of the time, talk to somebody who is having a panic attack, and you will see that their psyche will grab onto anything to guarantee a place in existence. Watch somebody who is dying, and who doesn't want to, their psyche will be grabbing at anything to give it a sense of self-survival, and as they leave the body, they are ready to grab their next body, and on and on it goes. The illusionary "I" is always trying to perpetuate its own self existence until one day it is seen through. So, people can have the sense of past lives, memories, and thoughts around the "I" but ultimately as this is worked through we see that there is no "I" and there never was. But sometimes when feeling caught, this necessitates going back into the deep past so we can find freedom now. And one day we can even see that past, present and future are contained in the now. So, all of this past healing is really a healing of this moment.

CHAPTER 21
Intra-uterine Trauma: The Pain of Being Born

The reality of intra-uterine trauma and birth pain points to the healing potential of the groundbreaking work of Stanislav Grof on the dynamics of the perinatal matrices.[1] Grof laid out four perinatal matrices in a progression through the birth process that captures the essence of the death and rebirth process. The key here is that a fully grown person's emotional pain can be actually caught up in the trials and tribulations of the birth process and these repressed experiences can be unconsciously guiding them in day-to-day life.

The first matrix is of the "original symbiotic unity of the fetus with the maternal organism at the time of intrauterine existence. During episodes of undisturbed life in the womb, the condition of the child can be close to ideal."[2] Grof described how this undisturbed intra-uterine state can be accompanied by experiences that share with it a lack of boundaries and images such as the consciousness of the ocean, an aquatic life form such as a whale, fish, or jellyfish, or interstellar space. Grof also described images of nature at its very best, beautiful, safe, nourishing, or even heavens or paradises symbolizing different cultures around the world. There are also elements of cosmic unity or mystical union.

Disturbances of intra-uterine life are associated with images and experiences of underwater destruction, polluted streams, contaminated nature, and insidious demons. The mystical rapture is replaced by psychotic distortion with paranoid undertones.[3] I have had clients describe to me very vividly a sense of a contaminated poisonous substance suddenly appearing all around them, making it very hard to feel safe. In one case, the mother was drinking alcohol during her pregnancy. It is hard to feel a basic trust with existence when already poisoned with alcohol with the accompanying impact on physiological development.

The second perinatal matrix is related to the onset of biological delivery and its first clinical stage. Grof described the difficulty of this stage:

> Here the original equilibrium of the intrauterine existence is disturbed, first by alarming chemical signals and then by muscular contractions. When this stage fully develops, the fetus is periodically constricted by uterine spasms; the cervix is closed and the way out is not yet available.[4]

Grof described the symbolic concomitant of the onset of this stage as being cosmic engulfment. There is overwhelming anxiety and awareness of an imminent vital threat in which the source of the danger can be readily identified. Typical imagery of this stage is the experience of a three dimensional spiral, funnel, or whirlpool, sucking the subject relentlessly towards its centre. An animal equivalent is being swallowed by a terrifying monster such as a giant dragon, python, crocodile or whale.

The symbolic counterpart to this stage is the experience of "no exit or hell." Grof described this hell as "a sense of being stuck, caged, or trapped in a claustrophobic, nightmarish world and experiencing incredible psychological and physical tortures. The situation is usually absolutely unbearable and appears to be endless and hopeless. The individual loses the sense of linear time and can see no possible end to this torment or any form of escape from it."[5] Experiential links are obvious here. This can produce experiential identification with prisoners in dungeons or concentration camps, inmates in insane asylums, sinners in hell or archetypal figures symbolizing eternal damnation. Here in this hell, one can lose track of anything positive in the world and existence as profound metaphysical feelings of helplessness, hopelessness, inferiority, despair, and guilt arise. Overall, it is a feeling of experiencing a destructive force with no chance of escaping. A person talking about being suspended in perpetual darkness may actually be accessing the memory of a painful childbirth in which she or he was suspended for many hours in the "no exit or hell" phase.

In the third perinatal matrix, Grof described how the territory changes:

> The uterine contractions continue, but unlike in the previous stage, the cervix is now dilated and allows a gradual propulsion of the fetus through the birth canal. This involves an enormous struggle for survival, crushing mechanical pressures, and often a high degree of anoxia and suffocation. In the terminal phases of the delivery, the fetus can experience intimate contact with such biological material as blood, mucus, fetal liquid, urine, and even feces.[6]

The experiential point of view involves a wide variety of phenomena that include elements of a titanic fight, sadomasochistic experiences, intense sexual arousal, demonic episodes, and encounter with fire all in the context of a death-rebirth struggle.

The epic struggles make sense if we think of the frail baby's head wedged in a narrow pelvic opening by the power of uterine contractions that oscillate between fifty and one hundred pounds. It can feel like raging elements of nature such as volcanoes, storms, earthquakes, tidal waves or tornadoes, violent scenes of war or revolution or high powered technology such as bombs and nuclear reactors. Related themes include images of the feats of superheroes, and mythological battles of cosmic proportion involving demons and angels or gods and titans. There can be sadomasochistic aspects of this matrix such as bloody sacrifice, self-sacrifice, torture, execution, murder, sadomasochistic practices, rapes and experiences that combine sex with death around experiences of suffocating and inhuman suffering. There also can be related themes of the Witches' Sabbath, satanic orgies or Black Mass rituals.[7]

The experiential pattern of this matrix has a whole different feel to it than the previously described no-exit constellation. The situation is much closer to purgatory, and the person is not just in the role of a helpless victim, and at times might be difficult to distinguish between whether the person is the hero or the victim. The whole death–rebirth struggle is on the borderline between agony and ecstasy and the fusion of both. Grof described this stage as volcanic ecstasy as opposed to the ocean ecstasy of the cosmic union highlighted in the first stage.[8]

Finally, the fourth perinatal matrix is related the third clinical stage of delivery and that is the actual birth of the child. Grof laid it out:

> In this final stage, the agonizing process of the birth struggle comes to an end; the propulsion through the birth canal culminates and the extreme build-up of pain, tension, and sexual arousal is follow by a sudden relief and relaxation. The child is born and, after a long period of darkness, faces for the first time the intense light of the day (or the operating room). After the umbilical cord is cut, the physical

separation from the mother has been completed and the child begins its new existence as an anatomically independent individual.[9]

If allowed to happen, the transition from the third perinatal matrix to the fourth involves a sense of annihilation on all imaginable levels—physical, emotional, intellectual, ultimately moral failure, and an absolute damnation of transcendent proportion. This is a merciless destruction of all previous reference points for the individual. Grof described how after this experience of total annihilation and of hitting cosmic bottom, this can be immediately followed by visions of blinding white or golden light of supernatural radiance and beauty, or associated, astonishing displays of divine archetypal entities, rainbow spectra, or intricate peacock designs, or cloudbursts or reawakened nature in spring. Here the subject feel a deep sense of spiritual liberation, redemption, and salvation, and typically feels freed from anxiety, depression, and guilt. With a flood of positive emotions, towards self, others, and existence, the world appears to be a beautiful and safe place.[10]

My Own Observations of the Perinatal Matrices

With all of my intense trauma work that I had already completed, including catharsis, psychodrama, choiceless awareness, acceptance of death, and past life trauma, I have seen parallel themes with intrauterine trauma. I have enjoyed much time in wondrous meditations and doing nothing but sitting in the blissful cosmic ocean of existence which is similar to the first womb phase. I have done a sitting in total darkness with my eyes open meditation for many years which seemed very similar to the second matrix with its themes of no exit and a dark world of sinister permanent engulfment. As I sat in the darkness, the horror melted and turned into love. All my work in primal therapy and catharsis and learning to not judge any trauma or hell realm experience seemed to capture the agony of the third matrix and the cosmic battle to be born in a sea of both light and sinister forces. Letting go of the need to survive and dropping the discriminating mind, meant I had transcended beyond the good and evil epic battle of the third matrix. Total surrender and death— and then finding the light in darkness of non-existence— seemed to capture the fourth matrix of going through annihilation to be born into the light. It seemed that these perinatal matrices nicely captured the death–rebirth process that I already worked through in many other ways.

I have realized that working through unresolved issues in these matrices can be very helpful to people. I look for signs with clients that indicate this is where they may need to go. Disturbances in the womb such as a mother drinking may have implications for a sense of basic trust as the unconscious bliss of the first matrix could never be really enjoyed. Hearing a client talk about a long and drawn out birth of ten hours is an indication that the client may have spent an extended time in the no exit of matrix two and the cosmic battle phase of matrix three. Hearing a client talk constantly about death, and how maybe he or she should not have even been born, may mean that he or she is still psychologically caught in the death–rebirth cycle of being born.

People can re-experience the birthing process as well as other cosmological themes of existence through Grof's Holotropic Breathwork Therapy. The therapy uses evocative music and accelerated breathing to access the perinatal states. Grof has trained facilitators available around the world.[11]

CHAPTER 22
Hell Realm Trauma: From Enduring Terror to Finding the Light Within the Darkness

In the previous chapters, we looked at a traumatic death from a previous life and the passage through no-exit of the birth process. In this chapter, we are going to dive in further to explore the apparent hell realm aspect of existence. It is evident there can be an experience of psychic hell realm fates far worse than death. This is where a non-dual journey can go awry if it is not worked through. As Adi Da articulated, it is the prolonged torment that can be so frightening as it seems to go forever:

> At the level of the psyche, it is not so much a fear of dying, because there is a presumption of continuousness that is not so strongly present at the physical level. The fear at the level of the psyche is fear of certain conditions, fear of madness, fear of being confronted by terrifying phenomena. At the physical level you fear termination of physical life. At the psychic level you fear madness and confinement by unchanging terribleness. ... In the psyche, you fear being confronted not by pain and mortality, which are features of fear at the physical level, but by

torment, dissociation, horrors of all kinds, bewilderment, and loss of relations.[1]

Adi Da has effectively captured the utter terror of the psychic hell realm. At the psychic level, when we encounter "hell" experiences, the ardent desire is not so much to survive, as you may be facing permanently being stuck in hell. The urgency is more to escape the predicament. I want to get the hell out of hell!

Renz wrote about his predicament dealing with the prospects of experiencing an eternal hell realm as he was gripped by the unfolding story of Yuddhistra and Krishna played out in a TV program. The essential piece of the story centres upon the aftermath of a bloody battle and the death of Yuddhistra. Upon his death, wanting to join his family and friends, Yuddhistra saw his loved ones burning in hellfire and suffering eternally. At this moment, Yuddhistra fell into total despair and the poignant question was asked by Krishna as to whether or not Yuddhistra could remain in that condition forever. Renz recalled:

> By this time I was so deeply involved in the play and so completely identified with Yuddhistra that I felt the question was actually addressed to me. He, or I, answered, "I have no desire to change anything or to avoid pain or suffering. If I must remain in this condition for the remainder of my existence, so be it."... at this moment an explosion-like experience tore through the back of my head, filling my perception with pure light. At this moment, there was an absolute acceptance of being. Time stopped, ... and the world disappeared, and a kind of pure *Is-ness* in a glaring light appeared. It was a pulsating silence, and absolute aliveness that was perfect in itself—and I was that.[2]

This description is not foreign to me. I, too, have had to confront the psychic horror that a terrible existence may go on forever. Similar to Yuddhistra and Renz's predicament, I had been seeking long-term, looking for a way out of my experience in existence, to some escape into a sanctuary. But like Renz, I have come to see that there is no escape, in that we are part of existence forever. There is no place to go!

This, at first blush, seems like an awful fate, that there is no escape. But if one lets it in, that there is no escape from existence, then one accepts there is no way out of this predicament. We are in existence in one way or another forever. In seeing that nothing can be done, a person relaxes. And the eternal radiant light of existence shines through. That was my own experience. There was no point struggling to find a way out because there is no way out. Here there is no escape, so I might as well just relax and take it easy. No way out—if accepted—means relaxation.

And as one lets go of escaping, a new realization emerges. I realized it was not the situation *per se* that was so awful, it was intense struggle to escape. I realized the only thing to do was to accept hell, give up my struggle, and accept there is no way out. So, like Renz, the question was "Was I willing to be in hell forever?" The answer was yes. And with that deep acceptance, my so-called hell realm instantly transformed into brilliant light.

Reflecting on this transformational acceptance, it appeared obvious to me that this hell was just the ordinariness of existence, absolute presence, and eternal aloneness. It had just been magnified in my desire to escape the so-called *hell* experience. Through acceptance of no escape, the eternal misery turns to an eternal mystery. When the dark-side-of-the-moon experience is accepted, a total bedazzlement can open up. When it is accepted that there is no way out of existence, and one accepts eternal citizenship, the horror can transform into blissful light, a bedazzling mystery.

The Bardo Realm of Hell: Compacted Aggressiveness

There is the hell of no escape and eternal banishment in which one feels stuck in their predicament forever. I would be remiss if I left the discussion of hell at that. Existence is manifold, levels upon levels. There can be an experience of hell which seems to be a very low frequency area in which existence is reduced to its most base element. Trungpa, in discussing the bardo realm of hell, calls it the realm of total aggression in which there is no spaciousness and it is very claustrophobic.[3] This is reminiscent of psychiatrist David Hawkins work on consciousness frequency.[4] A hell experience may be that we are vibrating at the most base level of existence, the most aggressive primal punitive frequency, beings are lost in a primal instinctual grasping at survival. If you are reduced to this level through a bad drug trip, a scary near death experience, exhaustion or a crashing into a dark psychotic episode, a key theme is that you are hanging on, desperate to survive no matter what. This is an invitation to surrender, to give up the fight and trust existence. Let go of fear and fighting, surrender.

Taking the Trauma out of Hell: Realizing There is Nobody in Charge

To bring greater clarity to the healing of dark hellish experiences within the psyche, one just has to re-remember that there is no ultimate goal in existence. There is nowhere to go, and nothing to be done. Now, if we look closely, we can see that having a goal sets up division between the virtuous and the sinners, between heaven and hell. Creating the goal creates the division of those bound for heaven and those bound for hell. With no goal, the ground of all of this disappears. One is not going anywhere. There is nowhere to go and *nobody* to go. All is always right here and has always been available.

Religion depends on a single phenomenon, disobedience. If you obey, you are going to heaven, and if you disobey, you are going to hell. But if we can see that there is no goal, then we also can see that there is nobody to command, and there is no one to obey. All the hierarchical structure falls away. The prison of hell and heaven falls away, and we are left with the suchness of existence.

If we take away all the formal hierarchies of heaven and hell, we notice that existence has a whole multitude of levels of vibrational frequencies. There is no point hanging out at a very primal hell aggression level, as not much can happen at that level of frequency. There is just compacted aggressiveness, no space, and everything is almost compressed to concrete. So in deconstructing *hell*, we are simply pointing out the realities of participating in existence at a very low level of vibrational intensity.

We can integrate all levels; we do not necessarily want to get stuck in any one place. For example, through hell realm experience, it can be realized that there is a brute level of aggression that needs to be integrated, as it is part of existence. It could be useful sometime. Adolph Hitler and the Nazis needed to be met with brute aggression in World War II to stop the genocide of Jewish people and to stop them from taking over the whole world. My wife's father ran like a madman and escaped a Nazi prison camp as an allied soldier. If you are attacked by a grizzly bear hiking, you are going to have to embrace animal aggressiveness very fast. The point is that we may need to access this level of vibration; we just we don't want to get stuck at this level—we simply need to be aware that existence can play out at this vibrational level of brute aggressiveness.

Integrating Black Hatred

An important transformational key is the realization that we can integrate qualities of total blackness, what could be called the Beast, by not projecting them outside ourselves, but finding them within ourselves through our black hatred and our accompanying cold destructiveness, as laid out by Almaas:

> When you allow the black hatred is when you feel yourself become the devil—a giant, black and powerful demon with tremendous pride and destructive hatred. You might tower over the city, looking at it and laughing. You might be filled with a powerful, destructive, cold, calm, and calculating hatred.[5]

The paradox is that, if this hatred can be felt with acceptance, it can transform all by itself to essential power.

The way this can work is through letting a person express this deep hatred openly. Many times in the non-dual group process, when it has come up, I have encouraged group members to express their deep hatred not only to absent family members but to the group as a whole, or group members, or to me personally. I remember one time, an addictions counsellor group member, Kevin, dropped into hatred towards me, and I encouraged him to let me have his hatred full throttle. He went at me hard, with an over the top intensity, screaming loudly about how much he hated my guts. I remember looking over at him while he was screaming at me, seeing his wild dark black eyes as if they were a wild black storm. He went at it hard for about ten minutes. I did nothing. After the storm abated, I asked him how he was doing.

"I feel great," he said, "so empowered." And then he said a funny thing to me. "I love you."

I smiled to myself. By being able to wildly express his hatred, he had found love. Essential blackness accepted, transformed to love. Beautiful!

Hell is Nowhere to Be Found

Thus, overall, we can see the so-called *Hell* experience can be deconstructed through accepting no escape and accepting and integrating our own repressed primal aggressiveness and hatred. We see that there is no objective hell as we relax into the light within the darkness and find "hell" is nowhere to be found. Like with so much of our darkness transformational work, an important insight is that trying to survive no matter what is what perpetuates apparent hell. Since I have moved to embrace the art of dying, and acceptance of death in each moment, "Hell" has disappeared. In letting go of grasping at survivalhood in each moment, I can relax and enjoy the translucent energy of existence in each moment. Paradoxically, the other side of this, is letting go of the need to escape, I can embrace the eternity of existence right here, right now.

Thus, it is just a total relaxation into vast no-selfhood. It is clear that "hell" can't be found anywhere. All is just a play of existence.

PART SIX

Embracing the Bedazzling Mystery

The radiant flowering of stillness is unexplainable as it is beyond you or me. It is a flowering of existence. The separate self has to die to existence for stillness to flower; as long as there is somebody there, there is somebody exerting effort or managing stillness. Desiring awakening or stillness is still just desire, a mortgage on the present moment for the future. When all desire is seen through, the illusion of the separate self dissolves. With this, we realize there is nowhere to go and nothing to do. We relax and stillness reveals itself.

But what is required these days is much more. Awakening needs to keep evolving, and it is clear that resting on top of the mountain or embracing the passive void is no longer enough. What is called for, now, is to come down and share our awakening and all encompassing love with everything in life: with our friends, family, institutions, communities, and the whole globe. We rest in no-knowing innocence and reside in non-conceptual awareness, and yet, can let existence reveal its secrets. We plunge into new creations and arisings that emerge from this wondrous place of being. We are hollow bamboos of non-doing doing so that the lightning radiance of active infinity can shine through. All of this frees us to enjoy the eternal dance, the eternal play of existence. Always transcending ourselves as we realize this journey never stops, we joyously embrace this wondrous existence, and celebrate this infinite bedazzling mystery.

CHAPTER 23
Ordinary and Joyously Useless: Just to Be Is Enough

Only Nobodies are Awakened

Awakening and enlightenment appear to represent the finest in human experience, the radiance of existence shining through the human form. There is the apparent extraordinariness of awakening, but even that has to be let go of because at the heart of awakening is the recognition that one is a nobody, an ordinary nobody. All sense of specialness drops, the ego dissolves, and in nobody-ness, one is surrendered to existence. Ambition has been dropped, and emptiness is embraced in the sky of awareness. The inner emptiness connects with the outer emptiness, and the full emptiness of form and formless is sublimely enjoyed. It is both blissful and very ordinary as it is available to all. It is nothing special. When we tune in we see that existence itself is enlightened.

I frequently use the expression "poking along in eternity," to signify the enlightened state in which one is relaxed and there is a recognition that there is no place to get to, nothing particular to do, it is all available right here, right now. But all of this is very ordinary, as no special claims can be made for something that is available to all. The ego may have been attracted to the so-called specialness of "awakening" in the beginning, but that ego has long ago been burnt through.

Just to Be

It is quite ironic that, after so much seeking and trauma healing, just to *be* is enough. The eternal now is not something done, the eternal now happens. After all of the techniques and methods, it is apparent that just to *be* is enough, nothing else is needed. Everything under the sun has been done, and it is obvious that existence is not something that has to be grown into, it is already there, it is already the case—relaxation happens.

Relaxation is not a method; it is just an understanding that nothing is to be done, so effort disappears. This ordinary life of working, loving, and connecting is embraced. Extraordinariness is not needed. I teach my classes, run my groups, do my writing, go for my long runs, connect with my wife.

The mysteriousness of existence and the beautiful translucent light of existence shows up on its own, no management is necessary. Just poking along in the ordinariness of existence is enough as everything is revealed.

Dark Valleys are a Dream

Abiding in this "poking along" way of being brings the realization that so-called dark valleys and nightmares of life are a dream. All of the time spent working through the blackest darkness was only needed so that the light within the darkness could be revealed. Reality reveals a beautiful mystery in which the blackness interconnects with light, death intersects with life, the emptiness is a full aliveness, and all of existence is radiant with a translucent shimmer. Contradictory aspects of life have become complementary.

Now with the discriminating mind set aside, *what is success* and *what is failure* falls away. It is all just a happening; effortless non-doing doing unfolds as the energy of the absolute flows through this apparent individual.

Joyously Useless

Functioning for the purpose of survival has fallen away. Personal will has been replaced by the absolute flowing through. From this place of nothing to do, most activity falls away. But what does arise is carried out with intensity as the energy of existence resonates through this apparent being. I am joyously useless and celebrate sauntering along in existence with no place to get to. While, I receive many invitations to be useful for people, go to dinners, help with research, teach extra lectures, I stay with my uselessness and respond from there. I have given up trying to be a success, a hero, and instead poke along enjoying each moment. I accept failurehood as I can only offer to others the invitation for transformation; the invitation to see into their own fundamental nature. In accepting failurehood, there is room for the impossible to happen.

Touch and Let Go

Each moment is embraced with no grabbing, and letting go happens. Existence is once again fresh in this moment. There is no point making deals to ensure survival into the next moment, as life is dangerous in each moment, and no one knows what is going to happen next. The insecurity of existence is accepted as the open sky of insecurity. The person I connect with totally in this moment, may totally go the other way the next day. The person that professes love for me now, may move into anger in a few minutes. The secure job today becomes a budget cut the next month. The dangerousness of existence is accepted. It is a fact of existence. Existence is celebrated in this moment with the realization that there is nothing to grab onto for the next moment. Death could show up at any time, and I am ready.

CHAPTER 24
Embracing Imperfection

There is no perfect landing place of awakening that provides a sanctuary forever, as on and on this journey goes. In each moment of existence, everything is afresh. I like Loch Kelly's expression for this: *the plane never lands*.

When Osho was asked, "Can an enlightened person become unenlightened again?" he responded, "When the ripe fruit has fallen off the tree, there is no way for that fruit to jump back on the tree again."[1] The Buddha pointed to a perfect, utmost enlightenment, "the absolute exalts the holy person" he called it.[2] It is apparent that something wonderful has happened, yet, at the same time, obvious shadow issues with people who are in so-called "perfect, utmost enlightenment" can be seen. Could *both* perspectives be right? Is possible for an individual to awaken and be liberated into the vastness of existence and yet still have unresolved shadow issues? Isn't it always a process? No matter how awakened a person claims to be, the potential for shadow issues in each moment is perhaps always there.

At a recent non-dual conference I hosted, one presenter bravely talked about her experience of being a non-dual teacher yet having to recognize her co-dependent patterns with her daughter who had chronic addictions issues. Despite all of her non-dual awakening, training, and healing, for many years she still found herself co-dependently pulled into the plight of her daughter's addiction. Byron Katie calls this being on the wrong side of the street, going over to the other side of the street and being in somebody else's business.[3] Being authentic means recognizing issues that have come up in awareness even after non-dual awakening.

Zen Master Dennis Genpo Merzel identified these hidden shadow issues that arise after awakening as akin to being "stuck in the absolute." He developed a process to address and integrate these hidden issues into what he calls "the True Self," which includes and transcends the dual and the non-dual self.[4] He outlines three stages involved in moving to abiding in non-dual being, which he calls the "great enlightenment" or "dropped-off-body-mind" or "the great liberation". More significantly, he delineates what happens in a further fourth stage:

> So what happens is now the self comes in, in a covert way as a disowned voice. The experience is no-self, but then what happens is the ego takes that experience, owns that experience, and then walks around saying, "I have no ego, I have no self."… That's why stage four is so important and so difficult, because no one is going to go to stage four. Because stage four is returning to embrace the self, it's returning to the dual and to the personal—in other words the self comes back, OK?[5]

Merzel calls this stage 4, "Falling from Grace" because it's like Humpty Dumpty sitting on a wall and then Humpty Dumpty does a face plant… does a face plant, right? …right into the pavement and shatters."[6]

So, most of who have awoken into non-dual being need to be prepared for a Stage Four in which we "Fall from Grace." We need to let the humanity of this fall in. For me, my fall from grace was tied up with heightened energy to be on the edge of discovery, on the very frontier of human consciousness, helping shape the next step in human consciousness development. However, I did not own this impulse directly, and it would come out with an over-the-top intensity, and I would create far more resistance than openness in others. At times it seemed to border on crazy wisdom and not the good kind.

So, rather than disowning this part of myself, I had to take a good close look at it. There seemed to be a helpful intention behind it, in that I envisioned a whole new development of understanding of non-duality, but I seemed to let this intensity come out only at a few isolated times, in a piecemeal fashion. Finally, one time, after a few turbulent days of stepped-up intensity, my wife said to me:

"Why don't you just own this part of yourself in day-to-day life; the need to be way out there on the creative edge? Embrace it directly, head on, and go for what you are truly interested in."

I remember thinking, *Hmmmph...* It seemed like a good point. There was a part of me that just loved being out in no person's land, treading new territory for human existence, why not just integrate it and make it a big part of my life?

Since that time, a number of years ago, when I acknowledged that aspect of being and accepted and integrated it, there has been a huge shift in my life. As a result, I started a non-dual psychology peer reviewed journal, started hosting a non-dual psychology conference every year, wrote many non-dual journal articles, and *this*, of course, is my second book. So, for me it was important to recognize the part that wanted to be on the edge of the unknown, far gone into wildness, and give it room to be expressed in everyday life. It has become a way of truly following my bliss.

Merzel has made some astute connections on how owning the disowned human aspect can actually open up Big Heart in addition to Big Mind. Merzel explains:

> Big Mind is basically not an active thing—it's a process of awareness and consciousness; its beingness. Big Heart is actually then coming back into the body and eventually return to the marketplace, right? …For me, returning to the marketplace doesn't mean just going back into the city and working—it means coming back to the market owning all the disowned aspects that we have disowned when we became spiritual. Like when we became spiritual, obviously we pursue loving and compassion more that we do hatred and bigotry; we disown all of these things that we consider not spiritual, right? We try to be more compassionate, more loving, more kind, more considerate, more generous, more open; and we disown all the opposites. So returning to the marketplace is re-owning all those aspects but not being controlled by them; being the masters. In other words, if I get angry, the anger is usually very much connected to what we would call wisdom; it's coming from wisdom. It's compassion coming out of the wisdom of the non-dual, in the dualistic realm, in the world, in the marketplace.[7]

With greater acceptance, I could see that my over-the-top intensity relating to new developments in the non-dual field was coming from a place of wisdom. Rather than denying and attempting to control the impulse to push the frontiers of non-dual being and understanding, I needed to accept it and bring it into day-to-day life, by letting existence flow through this mind–body and put these new arising developments out into the world. The answer was certainly not to hide and think *I can't put new things out there*. That would merely have stifled me and led to a lack of integration and inevitable falls from grace, when that leading edge voice would come out sideways. In short, step out of the way and let existence flow through spontaneously.

I have carried on with this emphasis in my non-dual counselling and psychotherapy work. We all can do face plants and fall from grace. It certainly does open up the Big Heart, for one realizes even with so-called non-dual awakening, disasters and huge mistakes can happen, and the lessons from this need to be owned and integrated. The learning process goes on and on as we integrate our lessons and give back to the community and keep opening up to the vaster planes of existence.

CHAPTER 25
Relaxing into Sublime Stillness

When we let go of striving and goal seeking as we realize that there is nowhere to go, and nothing to do, we can relax into the cosmic simultaneity of it all. Here a person can just embrace existence, let go and be one with all. Here one see that there is nobody higher or lower: all of existence the minerals and rocks, the trees and flowers, the animals and people are all part of this vast existence. Comparison is not needed; all is embraced.

And with the relaxation of goals and desires, a person simply slows down, for there is no place to go. Life is now here. And in this place of now here, a new world reveals itself, one of infinite friendship and kinship with all of existence from the trees to the ocean to the all of the animals, and all of people in humankind. As a person relaxes in this place of letting go of all ego ideals and simply enjoying the what is of existence, the vast sublime stillness of existence reveals itself. The perfect sublime stillness of existence, *Sat-Chit-Anand*, truth consciousness bliss is embraced.[1]

Sat-Chit-Anand does not come in parts. It is one unitive cosmic orgasmic experience. It is a subjective radiance of the utter blissful joy of existence. There is no concern with the other as all is embraced as one. It is just an utter enjoyment of the sublime blissful stillness of existence. This is not the stillness of effort, discipline or technique; this is the stillness that reveals itself when personal goals and desires are let go of. A person is no longer grinding away towards the future, and existence is embraced now so that the beautiful stillness can reveal itself. The old Zen expressions says "the grass grows by itself" and we see, with stillness, that certainly is the case, for we do not have to do anything but just get out of the way and stillness comes as a gift of existence as it is already here.

People *try* to *be still*. Effort and the array of different meditation techniques they force upon themselves all end up in total failurehood because they are trying to get to stillness through effort which implies desire. As long as there are desires at play in the mind, the mind can never be still, for the mind is obsessed with realizing its goal in the future. The mind is spinning away with strategies to achieve its goal, and making a goal out of stillness is simply another desire for the mind to pursue. Stillness forced upon by the mind will truly only be forced quietness and does not have the radiant vastness of true surrender and stillness.

Stillness arises out of understanding not out of some sort of technique. As long as there are desires to be obtained in the future, the mind will be tense and unable to be at rest, for the mind is preoccupied with whether it can obtain its goal or not. When one looks at the nature of desire, one sees it always a horizon in the future, trying to obtain some goal in the future. The problem is that *this moment* is rejected as not being good enough, and the desire is pursued for the future. But one can see how crazy this is, for this moment is all you actually have. So, in desire one is rejecting this moment, for some future moment which never comes—when it comes, it once again will be in this moment. When one sees the madness of this—how one could keep on rejecting this moment for some future moment on and on forever—the pattern drops. Now it becomes essential to celebrate this moment as that is all there is. One does not become desireless as the opposite of desire, as that would be a product of desiring desirelessness. Instead the whole pattern of grabbing onto desire drops away.

It can be shocking to look around. Everybody is chasing dreams of one kind or another. Some are chasing money, others prestige, higher education, excitement, sex, power, relationships, on and on it goes. Everybody is chasing. Some are even chasing awakening, freedom and enlightenment.

The idea that there is some place to get to has to be dropped. It needs to be seen that nothing has to be done—stillness arises not through effort but through *understanding*. You can't follow another to stillness. If seeking and desire are dismantled, a person realizes that there is nothing to be realized, nothing to be known, nothing to do, and nowhere to go. This moment is enough, this moment is eternity. A person can simply relax into this.

With relaxing into "this", into the "what is" of existence, the brilliant ecstatic stillness of existence reveals itself. The bedazzling mystery opens up. All of this arises through no effort, just a relaxing into existence. In the eternity of this moment, stillness reveals itself. The luminous magical sublime quality of existence dances and shimmers in the moment. From here, one sees the birth of so many Zen haikus that capture the dazzling poignant beauty of the play of form in stillness in this moment. Ordinary experiences become intensely captivating such as coming upon a very still deer on a coulee running trail, looking into a friendly dog's brown eyes, a purple and red sunset, a dark rich morning coffee.

The whole process of awakening has been one of a change of occupancy. We have become one with existence, and in stillness, the ecstasy and beauty of existence reveals itself to the nobody that is now here.

The Iridescent Beauty

Here in stillness there is an invitation to go beyond Sat-Chit-Anand (truth-consciousness-bliss). Three words from the ancient sources are *Satyam, Shivam, Sundram*[2] which mean "Truth, Goodness, Beauty." We have truth, but more than that for in "Shivam" we have the action of virtue, the action of goodness, the action of love, the action of pure godliness. A person is sharing the truth and love of existence in action. Stillness is shared with others through a combination of spoken words and being. The truly impactful teachers have had this quality. Even though coming from a place of stillness, they have been able to share it with others through a combination of words, love and beingness.

Stillness points to a third quality—*beauty*. The greatest beauty is to see and experience the wondrous beauty of the totality, the flowering in existence of consciousness itself, the bedazzling mystery.

Here is where we see that sitting in stillness is not only abided in but shared with fellow beings. In the embracement of stillness through action, a person naturally takes on a function of spreading the stillness to other beings in existence. Every act is done with totality, all down to the most basic functions of the day—eating meals, sitting, going to bed—and this totality in acting radiates the beauty of existence in the moment. One sees this so vividly in messengers of stillness, their utter simplicity and ease in each moment as they saunter about their day, always total and mindfully aware, even in the smallest action in each moment. They become the living embodiments of the beauty of truth in their graceful surrender to existence in each moment. Here, something fascinating happens; others in the presence of this graceful embodiment of truth in each moment experience an elixir-like fascination that draws them towards this mysterious expression of existence which is something far beyond what words can convey.

CHAPTER 26
Seeing through the Desire for Non-dual Teacherhood

The desire for enlightenment is a trap because as long as the desire for enlightenment is there, enlightenment can never be found because one is still trying to get somewhere in the future. No manner of wonderful spiritual experiences, cosmic unitive experience, or wonderment will release me, as the *me* still desires enlightenment. What is *me* but desire? Me trying to get beyond the mind to some goal of enlightenment is just a strategy of the ego. As Adyashanti described about his whole journey, this ego striving is a whole recipe for failurehood, and the sooner, the better![1] When the desire for awakening dissolves through failurehood, the ego drops away, and existence reveals itself in this moment.

In my own experience, through absolute hopelessness and total failurehood, the ego dropped away and existence was embraced. I, however, was not prepared for a new set of problems. Through the awakening process, I naturally assumed the Bodhisattva vow, of after awakening helping all sentient beings come to awakening. After a while, though, similar to my desire for awakening, this wanting to help others awaken was a setup for misery as well. Wanting to help other beings find their original nature, is perhaps a noble desire, but it still is a desire. Desire impinges on the moment, as it is a tension of wanting something to happen in the future. Because I want to help people in the future, it is a tension now.

I could see that I was subtly waiting for more beings to show up so I could help them. That subtle waiting is a demand on existence in the moment; it is like a complaint, saying to existence "Where are all the people I want to work with?" I could see that, after a while, I had trapped myself once again with desire—the wanting to help others awaken—because it was a subtle way of saying to existence this moment is not good enough. I was rejecting this moment for some future preferred moment in which there would be more people for me to work with.

This awareness also made me check closely into some non-dual teachings, for I felt others must have experienced this problem as well. The Buddha's teachings in The Diamond Sutra point to the insight of nobody helping nobodies realize they are nobody:

> What do you think, Subhuti, does it occur to the Tathagata, "by me has Dharma been demonstrated"? Whosoever, Subhuti, would say, "the Tathagata has demonstrated Dharma", he would speak falsely, he would misrepresent me by seizing on what is not there. Because not even the least Dharma is there found or got at. Therefore it is called "utmost, right and perfect enlightenment". Furthermore, Subhuti, self-identical is that Dharma, and nothing is therein at variance. Therefore is it called "utmost, right and perfect enlightenment". Self-identical through the absence of a self, a being, a soul, or a person…What do you think, Subhuti, does it occur to a Tathagata, "by me have beings been set free"? Not thus should you see it, Subhuti! And why? There is not any being whom the Tathagata has set free.[2]

Here, the Buddha is basically saying there is nobody to be saved, freedom is everybody's nature. There is nothing to hang onto. The only thing that could be said is that there is an invitation, a reminder offered of what is already everyone's own nature. Nothing for the ego to grab onto.

Similarly, Bodhidharma said, "Buddhas don't save buddhas."[3] There can only be an invitation to realize your own nature, a reminder of who you already are. So, there is not much to grab onto here as to what is going on as it is very much like "selling water down by the river." A "teacher" is just a nobody pointing to what a person already is, another nobody.

For me, I knew this intellectually, but I had to see I was putting myself in suffering again with my inner demand to help people. That desire just made me miserable as it allowed my small brain–mind to get back in the driver's seat and strategize how to pull this off, what to do next? The whole rat race of mind and goal-setting had returned through the back door. When one sees clearly how, once again, one has been seduced by desire and pulled into the wheel of the mind, it just stops all by itself. It is just a complete falling away into being. It sure made me laugh as I realized even a noble desire can be a straight path to suffering.

The even crazier thing is that I was already working with many people on their non-dual journey; I just couldn't totally enjoy it as the mind was saying, *more… more… more*. It was a relapse back into mind. This made me laugh. It was so ordinary. I am an apparent non-dual person that seems to have to learn his lessons the hard way, through experience. So be it.

The way I look at it these days is that the mind with all of its expectations is dropped moment to moment. Expectations are misery, so cut the root. Whatever happens is what happens, and I will just totally enjoy writing and talking about non-dual being as a gift to existence. I am doing my thing. I drop the demand for the echo back and just surrender to existence and let the energy of existence dance through me like a hollow bamboo. There is no longer an expectation, as that just puts me in bondage, and I have been through that despair. I am just doing my thing: writing, talking, and facilitating non-dual groups. It is just a sharing of understanding.

I have also realized that I needed to drop the Bodhisattva vow of bringing all beings to nirvana. What I have noticed is that some beings want to have nothing to do with me, so that would be crazy to be attached to bringing them to nirvana. Instead, there is just an openness to work with beings who present themselves in my life, in one way or another. This helps me relax and enjoy totally who I do work with, with no demand to work with others or everybody. It seems that people who want to work with me just show up somehow. They decide they want to work with me, and we go from there. I like the simplicity of it. I like working with people who are desperate and at the end of the line. It only entails a small percentage of the non-dual population. That is beautiful!

Effortless Caring

Along with letting go of the desire of helping people to awakening, or the Bodhisattva vow of bringing all beings to nirvana, I have had to look deeply at "caring" or what I like to jokingly refer to as *pretending to care*. Trying to lead all beings to nirvana feels like a heavy load, and can lead to burnout. Being open to working with whoever shows up or the opportunities that present themselves can be light and playful. There is no mind involved, just a spontaneous reaction to what opens up in each moment. Then the whole energy changes from work and a burden to a celebratory sharing.

Letting go of the desire to help means, that for me, it is just a play of existence, letting existence flow through me like I am a hollow bamboo. I let go of the desire to be helpful, and I just surrender to existence and see what happens in each moment. It is play, and it is fun. I am no longer a small wave in existence trying to be helpful, but instead I have let go of this desire and let the ocean flow through me. The burden is gone. I have dropped my private will to be helpful and have embraced the cosmic will and let it flow through me. I am open to working with many people or nobody. All I can do is embrace existence in each moment and be open to whatever emerges. This means enjoying a non-dual group if there are six people or if there is a full group of twenty-five, it is all embraced. I am simply here to sing my song of the beauty of non-dual being and make some non-dual invitations. People can decide in their own way what they want to do with the pointers.

CHAPTER 27
Active Infinity, Passive Infinity

Rather than escaping the world by retreating into an idealized transcendent state, the sharing of our non-dual awakening needs to bring us back into the world. The awakening process is initially up into ascension and transcendence, then down through our bodies, and then out into the community. We need more than just the embracement of nothingness and passive compassion. We need to embrace no-self action as we bring our awakening back to our communities.

Many non-dual awakened traditions have encouraged awakened beings to actively embrace the misery and suffering of the world rather than just sitting in nothingness and passive compassion for the world. It is like the Buddhist meditation practice of breathing in the suffering of the world, absorbing it, and breathing out love and radiance. I have noticed, in my non-dual trauma work, that the healing potential over the last few years has really intensified, for when I work with clients in their trauma, I take on their suffering in the moment as well, so I am right with them. They feel my presence, and we work through a non-dual healing together. They feel more than just a passive presence, they feel an active presence working with them to unlock the trauma and move into non-dual essence. As my non-dual teacher friend Canella Michelle Meyers likes to call it the all inclusivity of the non-dual perspective. Everything is in fact workable.

We can expand this even further. The embracement of emptiness can be a celebration of a living emptiness in each moment in whatever aspect of life that presents itself. Rather than just a passive non-dual watching of existence, there can be an acceptance of existence and a play in all aspects. Rather than focusing on going beyond the point of return and the freedom of going beyond, there can be an active celebration of all aspects of life. It is like the Ten Bulls of Zen which did not stop at the eighth Bull of embracing nothingness, but pushed the limits all the way to the tenth Bull in which the person comes back to the marketplace and celebrates community ecstatically.[1]

The embracement of emptiness and form then extends to full living in the world. Thus, rather than just a passive non-involvement, the active infinite dance of existence can be embraced. This means a person can even take their non-dual presence into institutions, educational learning centres, even universities. The conflicts of these institutions do not need to be avoided. Myself, coordinating a bachelor and masters degree program in addictions and mental health counselling over the last fifteen years has offered a great training ground for non-dual energy to deal with all of the political, institutional, and individual self-centredness that goes on at a university. There are numerous opportunities with all the dynamics of professional turf wars and hardball academics—all great fun to enjoy from a non-dual perspective.

This acceptance, in an active way, of all levels of existence of course extends to relationships and families. I long ago killed my parents psychologically as Buddha recommended. And have totally embraced a non-dual perspective of touch and let go in my intimate relationship with a beautiful being, my wife. I have lovingly embraced being a stepfather to two daughters, Talis and Mikka, over the last twenty years. I transcend labels and experience my intimate family and friends, fellow non-dual sojourners, clients and students as fellow beings in existence.

I long ago realized that abiding in non-dual awakening in day-to-day life also meant not being afraid to incorporate non-dual being into my career path. With a PhD in Counselling Psychology focusing on transpersonal psychology, it seemed natural, as Joseph Campbell would say to "follow my bliss" and look for an opportunity in academia. When I landed my first college teaching job, I knew I was on my way. A year later, I had upgraded to a university professor's position in addictions counselling which incorporated a whole spiritual component. We can thank Bill Wilson's surrender experience and the following 12 step program for that. So, teaching addictions counselling at a university became a chance for me to follow my bliss, and as my emerging embracement of non-dual being ripened into clarity over time, I have been able to integrate a non-dual perspective into our addictions counselling bachelor program and now as well our recently established master's program in addictions and mental health counselling. I also have been able to obtain funding for non-dual research projects, started a non-dual psychology journal *Paradoxica* (paradoxica.ca), and host a yearly non-dual psychology conference at the University of Lethbridge. This is designed to bring the non-dual energy down to the level of institutions. Being on the outside, we can not make as much of a difference. Taking the risk of setting up non-dual informed programs within status quo institutions like a mainstream university allows us to really have an impact where it can count, and that is with the future counselling and therapy leaders of tomorrow.

People are always asking me, "How do you get away with utilizing a non-dual approach at a traditional university?" My response is that you have to be a bit of a trickster, in that the most important thing is that you have to at least appear to play by the apparent rules of the game. Time and time again, I have seen people think that what they are up to at the university is so innovative and special that they do not have to play by the rules—a big mistake. To embrace active infinity and embrace action through non-dual doing, even if we are in the most wonderful vast absolute space, we can't forget which context we are playing in. I like to look at this as being informed by an embodied non-dual perspective in that, as we embrace form in existence, we are attuned to the level of the game we are playing. For example, so much of being a university professor is based on the mirage of personal achievement, so I need to pretend to play that game to keep everything in play; if I don't, I am shown the door. So I keep writing and publishing peer reviewed journal articles.

Thus, it becomes obvious, as we embrace active infinity and let the absolute energy flow through us in action, we can not be naïve. We have to pay attention. Part of paying attention is recognizing when I have hit the upper ceiling phenomena. This means that when I have been promoting big changes at the institutional level, I need to recognize when the system's capacity for change has been overloaded, and it is starting to short out. It is the time to move into hovering for a while, before the whole system gets into some sort of knee-jerk reaction and tries to shut down the new innovative changes. I always liked what Lao Tzu said on the dangers of overwhelming success:

> Stretch a bow to the very full,
> And you will wish you had stopped in time.
> Temper a sword to its very sharpest,
> And the edge will not last long.
> When gold and jade fill your hall,
> You will not be able to keep them safe.
> To be proud with wealth and honor
> Is to sow the seeds of one's own downfall.
> Retire when your work is done,
> Such is Heaven's way.[2]

Embrace active infinity and then there comes a time to move back to passive infinity. Existence has its cycles. Active infinity embraced forever becomes madness. The music has been played and now there is a time for the nightsong of passive infinity, a resting before active infinity is embraced once again.

Tao: Letting Things Be

There can be a trap of always improving the world. Always being in an evolving process to improve the world means that we do not allow ourselves to relax and rest with what is. We do not enjoy the utter perfection of what is. Embracing the Tao action of non-action, wei-wu-wei, means we can let things be. The contemporary emphasis on constant economic and technological development is a future-oriented intentionality that is always interfering with the world.[3] In the place of spontaneity and natural creativity, we are always obsessed with organizing and improving the world. It is like we are always ascending and improving, but fail to recognize the natural joy of the Lao Tzu watercourse way of allowing ourselves to be water and relaxing into the lowest points of existence the way water does. We need to let ourselves naturally fold back into the unnamable Tao, the eternal feminine principle of existence with our roots in the lowest places so we can connect with all of existence.

These days, I see it as a movement between active and passive infinity, from non-dual doing to resting in stillness. It is a balance.

CHAPTER 28
Never Born, Never Died: The Ultimate Medicine

When we started the journey to awakening, we saw death as a big problem. It made us shudder, and was an invitation to wake up. When we got into the journey, we had to embrace the reality of our fundamental aloneness. We come into this world alone, we depart alone, and our fundamentally in our aloneness. But is that even true?

We embraced relatedness and then accepted our aloneness, both the paths of love and meditation. Ultimately, one needs to go beyond relatedness and aloneness, transcend either side of the spectrum, a worldly person or an other-worldy person. As Ikkyu says, "I will teach you the way. Not to come, not to go!"[1] This is the medicine of the unborn undying, what Nisargadatta called the "Ultimate Medicine."[2] In this place of suchness, we see that there is nothing to hang onto; there is just the vastness of existence with no death. Nobody comes and nobody goes. There is no longer anybody here to die. The body drops at physical death, but there is no death of the self as the self has long ago disappeared.

In my current life, I am no longer attached to whether I have a body or not; I have one now, but soon one day the body will be gone. Either way, I celebrate the bedazzling mystery of existence. The great cosmic joke, though, is that we have been beyond life and death all the way along, we just did not realize it as we were so attached to our body–minds. It is not an awareness that we need to attain, but something we just relax into as it is our own nature. It is mind-blowing to realize that our own nature is a gift of existence and not something that we need to strive towards with effort and discipline. We just can naturally and spontaneously embrace our own true nature. We embrace the art of dying in each moment. We let go of our attachment to our body–mind and discover our true nature in the beauty and intensity of this moment.

The true medicine for suffering lies in awakening to reality and "what is" as we realize there is no such thing as a permanent self, for in actuality no one exists. And as one goes deeper into this, one starts to enjoy what has been called the original or ultimate medicine and that is "never born, never died." We are the pure subjectivity of the vastness of existence that has always been here. In fact, rather than seeing that we are beings in time, we can see that time is in us. We were here in the beginningless beginning, and are here at the endless end. We are here in the eternal moment for eternity. As Karl Renz so intensely described in his book, *The Myth of Enlightenment*, "There is no escape."[3] When we realize there is nowhere to go, we can truly relax. We are one with existence.

Awakening in a Dream

As we relax into the ultimate medicine of "never born, never died," the mirage of a being becoming awakened becomes apparent. Papaji would sometimes humorously point this out:

> This is a dream. You've won Enlightenment in a dream! Wakeup and you will help everybody. "Other" will disappear, and "you" will disappear. The dreamer is no more. Wake up and tell me where the universe

and all its suffering and enjoyments are. Wake up and know you're not even created![4]

This ultimate medicine of awakening from the dream is a vast home of true relaxation. And from here, one can celebrate and see that nothing matters. One can see that it is all a game, for in this magic show of existence nobody actually exists. Osho in his Pune ashram use to look out at the ten thousand people that had gathered for one of his talks and say, "To you this seems real, but to me it is just a drama, a game of Master and disciple, and the day you see that will be your enlightenment. There is nobody here to become enlightened, and there is nobody here to be the Master."[5]

No Self, No Other

Seeing that nobody is here is a far more ordinary occurrence than many of us realize. It can arise quite naturally in everyday life. When I go for my daily hour run in nature, it is seen that there is nobody running, the body is just running by itself effortlessly in a commune with nature. This can easily extend to connections with others as well. For instance, when I teach a class of 60 students it is apparent nobody is here, just some apparent beings. When facilitating non-dual groups, it is obvious that there is nobody reminding other nobodies that they are nobody. This can ripen into a beautiful yet ordinary insight for many of my non-dual group participants. Suddenly, in the intensity of the moment, a group member will burst out in crazy laughter as it becomes obvious that there is no self, nor any other, there is just a vast interconnected energy in the moment. At times, it can seem that many of the group members are being swept away with this insight, and enjoying the ecstasy of the moment. The ongoing invitation becomes to relax into the vastness, yet at the same time enjoy the sacredness of embodied existence.

CHAPTER 29

Play: Enjoying the Dance and Love of Existence

Freedom is here and now. All of existence can be embraced in this moment in a celebration of formlessness and form. Rather than just a release from suffering and misery into a passive emptiness, a full emptiness can be celebrated in each moment. Rather than transcending into the beyond, the refreshing transcendence of the beyond can be brought down to the level of life lived and honoured in a full celebration of immanent energy and consciousness lived in the moment. We wake up, then we wake down back into our bodies, and then we wake out into our communities.

As the separate self is seen through and the change of occupancy takes place in that we start to live like a hollow bamboo with the vastness of existence flowing through us, it becomes apparent that life is a happening. Letting our managing minds go, we see that, in this moment, existence is just a grand play. Our private personal goals have been let go of, and now we are part of the cosmic will of existence. It is no longer serious work to be preoccupied with; instead we are enjoying the dance of existence. By letting go of our personal sense of self, we can see that, in this vast existence, there truly is a cosmic dance of abundant joy going on as clouds glide in the skies, rivers flow to the oceans, seeds become flowers, birds are on the wing, and love interconnects between men and women in a grand panoramic play of celebration and dance. There is truly an abundance of bliss in the heart of existence that is overflowing in this grand dance of planets, the sun and the moon, and the stars.

In this celebration of life—in the total dance of being and non-being—it is seen that each person has a role and act to play out in the moment. The apparent appearance of an individual is an act that can be taken on with zest. For example, I have long recognized that, to work at a university as a professor, it is important that I play out the role with total intensity.

I cannot start a counselling course by saying to the students:

"Ultimately there is nothing to know and no way to help another, so what are we even doing here?"

To do so would be to deconstruct my role before I even get started. No, I could see it was far better to play out the counselling professor role with zest. That way, one day, some of the students will get to the place of realizing there is nothing to know so they can just sit in being, but it is a process. So, in the meantime, I embrace my role, knowing it is a game that I can let go of in any moment.

Similarly, I let go of the results of my actions. All I can do is dive into actions with total intensity with no concern for the result. For example, each of my lectures is like my last class ever, so I radiate intensity and lay it on the line with no deals. Who knows, maybe it could be my last lecture? I could have a heart attack the same afternoon. Similarly this book is just a gift to existence; it might be read by ten people or by thousands. I leave that to existence. I do not wait for the mountain echo of this book, I make my shout through the mountain valley and leave the echo in the hands of existence.

I am like what Rinzai called himself: the man of no rank. I am a nobody with nothing to hang onto. I use to think I was a somebody, but long ago have let that go. I live in spiritual poverty in which I have nothing to hang onto, no experience, no possessions, no merit, no accumulated connections, and today might just be my last day in embodied existence. Death might just show up anytime, and I am ready to depart. I have seen through my importance in the grand scheme of things, and realize I am just a part of the play of existence. Just today, having coffee with two of my fellow faculty members, we were joking as to whom, upon my departure, is going to quickly lay claim to my office, and to all of my books. It is okay; I have already died, and have seen the dropping away of this body.

It is like what Lao Tzu says on knowing the Eternal Law:

> The myriad things take shape and rise to activity,
> But I watch them fall back to their repose,
> Like vegetation that luxuriantly grows
> But returns to the root (soil) from which it spring.
>
> To return to the root is Repose;
> It is called going back to one's Destiny.
> Going back to one's Destiny is to find the Eternal Law,
> To know the Eternal Law is Enlightenment.
> And not to know the Eternal Law
> Is to court disaster.[1]

Death is destiny, and so it is not the enemy of life, for all paths lead to death. Rather than fighting death, when death is accepted, many aspects of life are immediately transformed.

What is amazing is this: if death is accepted as part of life, then even enemies are accepted as part of friendship as the basic duality of life and death has been dissolved, being and non-being. All other dualities are resolved in the relaxed clarity of being beyond life and death. We rest clearly beyond smoke in the eternal now translucent light of existence. So, for example, even when a graduate student turned on me and laid a complaint to the department of graduate studies, suggesting that I was leading a cult of non-duality at the university, I rested in the relaxed light of accepting death and enjoyed the situation. The mind tried to tell me that I should go rushing over to the Graduate Studies office to defend myself, but instead I did nothing, as there was nothing to do. And the complaint dropped by itself. I enjoyed how this person projected darkness upon to me and labeled me as evil and that I needed to be fired. She thought she was doing the rightcous thing, even though it involved her making some stories up, and exaggerating things all to justify her position. I enjoyed the theatre of it all.

Rather than being afraid of death in each moment, a life lived with intensity means that death is embraced in each moment as one can see it is the innermost core of life. Death is accepted as sublime relaxation. It is accepted that I too am a dead person walking towards the gallows as that is the natural order of things.

Love Remains

Lao Tzu says:

> I have three treasures;
> Guard them and keep them safe.
> The first is Love.
> The second is, Never too much.
> The third is, Never be the first in the world.[2]

The first, *Love*, says it all, but we get caught. The second treasure, *Never too much*, points to the disease of overdoing, over trying, making effort to the extreme. Mind does not rest naturally in balance, in the middle, it loves taking things to the extreme. We are always overdoing. And for much of my life I was like that, always trying far too hard. And the problem is that I could not really embrace the simplicity of love because I was too busy trying. When all this trying and overdoing is given up, a person naturally comes to rest in the middle. And in the middle, in balance, a person is free to embrace love in each moment.

Along with embracing *Never too much* naturally comes the third treasure: *Never be the first in the world*. The ambition to be first in the world means a person is not at home, not exalted, still caught in the insanity of ambition. If you are striving in the spiritual world, you are still caught in the misery of ambition. But in this moment, who cares about being first? I can take risks, have the absolute work through me in new ways, be on a leading edge *perhaps*, but there is no need to compare, for we are all interconnected anyways. Being first is all complete nonsense involving comparison and striving. We are all interconnected in a circle, the first joins the last. And the paradox is that by simply embracing this moment, with all of its wonder and bedazzling mystery, there is sublime perfection just in that. This mind–body enjoys being out at the edge of existence, but at the same time I realize I am "a man of no rank" and like the watercourse way, I rest at the bottom of existence, open to all levels and beings.

In the end, this all points back to the first treasure: *Love*. Love is here—I am at the bottom of existence itself and so all beings are my friend. There was a time when I was trying to ascend to the top, but that got washed away in a landslide, and now I am relaxed as a nobody. I am at the back of the line. There was a time I fashioned myself as becoming a cosmic hero, but now I recognize I am a cosmic bum like everybody else. My vast love comes from the recognition that I too thought I was the answer. I too thought I was the first, and that got swept away like a falling star in the recognition that I too had become the narcissistic problem of individual owned "spirituality" and was swept back into the sea of ordinariness where I belonged. I have seen my own inner ugliness hanging onto specialness and, on my knees, surrendered. So, here I am, not the answer, but instead embracing the vast loving open sky of existence in each moment. We are all one vast interconnected energy in which nobody exists independently, and nobody is the answer. From here, connected to all beings and things, there is just love.

It is not like I have tried to be loving in this journey, it is all that I have left. Knowledge and knowing has disappeared into "no knowing", and my body is now a sacred object in my existence. Meditation has transformed into enjoying the *is-ness* of the moment. Understanding has dissolved into nothing to hang onto. Self-inquiry has been burnt through, leaving just openness, and when I look for self in this moment, I can't see it anywhere. All that remains is a celebration of the vast empty sky of existence and an ecstatic lovingness for all form remains. That such a brilliant and bedazzling mystery lay waiting at the heart of so much suffering is the paradox of darkness.

References

Introduction
1. See J. Krishnamurti, *The First and Last Freedom*, New York: Harper and Row, 1954.
2. A. H. Almaas, *Elements of the Real in Man: Diamond Heart Book One*, Boston: Shambhala, 1987.

Part 1 (opening)
1. A. H. Almaas, *Inexhaustible Mystery: Diamond Heart Book Five*, Boston: Shambhala, 2011, p.13.

Chapter 1
1. A. H. Almaas, *The Point of Existence: Transformations of Narcissism in Self-Realization*, Boston: Shambhala, 2001.
2. Patrick Carnes, *Don't Call It Love: Recovery from Sexual Addiction*, New York: Bantam, 1991.

Chapter 3
1. J. Krishnamurti, *Freedom from the Known*, New York: HarperCollins, 1969.
2. Nyogen Senzaki and Ruth Stroud McCandless (Eds.), *Buddhism and Zen*, New York: Philosophical Library, 1953.
3. Adyashanti, *The End of Your World*, Boulder, CO: Sounds True, 2008.
4. Adyashanti, *The End of Your World*, Boulder, CO: Sounds True, 2008.

Chapter 4

1. See June Singer, *Boundaries of the Soul: The Practice of Jung's Psychology (rev. ed.)*, New York: Random House, 1994.
2. Adyashanti, *The End of Your World*, Boulder, CO: Sounds True, 2008.
3. Byron Katie, *Loving What Is: Four Questions that Can Change Your Life*, New York: Harmony Books, 2002.
4. A. H. Almaas, *Inexhaustible Mystery: Diamond Heart Book Five*, Boston: Shambhala, 2011, p.30.

Chapter 5

1. J. Krishnamurti, *The First and Last Freedom*, New York: Harper and Row, 1954.

Chapter 6

1. See June Singer, *Boundaries of the Soul: The Practice of Jung's Psychology (rev. ed.)*, New York: Random House, 1994.
2. Cited in N. Foster & J. Shoemaker, *The Roaring Stream: A New Zen Reader*, Hopewell, NJ: The Ecco Press, 1996, p. 11.

Chapter 7

1. Trevor Leggett (ed.), *First Zen Reader*, Rutland, Vermont: Charles E. Tuttle, 1960.
2. Miriam Greenspan, *Healing Through the Dark Emotions: The Wisdom of Grief, Fear, and Despair*, Boston: Shambhala, 2003, p. 78.
3. A. H. Almaas, *The Point of Existence: Transformations of Narcissism in Self-Realization*, Boston: Shambhala, 2001.

Chapter 8

1. Stephen Wolinsky, *The Way of the Human: The Quantum Psychology Notebooks: Volume 2 The False Core and the False Self*, Capitola, CA: Quantum, 1999.

Chapter 9
1. Martin Heidegger, *Being and Time*, New York: Harper and Row, 1962.**
2. See P. D. Ouspensky, *In Search of the Miraculous*, New York: Harcourt, 1949.

Chapter 10
1. A. H. Almaas, *Spacecruiser Inquiry*, Boston: Shambhala, 2002.
2. Joseph Campbell, *Follow Your Bliss: Conversations with Bill Moyers*, Nashville, TN: Vanderbilt University, 1989.

Chapter 11
1. A. H. Almaas, *Elements of the Real in Man: Diamond Heart Book One*, Boston: Shambhala, 1987, p. 16.
2. J. Firman & A. Gila, *The Primal Wound: A Transpersonal View of Trauma, Addiction and Growth*, Albany, NY: State University of New York Press, 1997, p. 14-15.
3. Miriam Greenspan, *Healing Through the Dark Emotions: The Wisdom of Grief, Fear, and Despair*, Boston: Shambhala, 2003.
4. A. H. Almaas, *Elements of the Real in Man: Diamond Heart Book One*, Boston: Shambhala, 1987, p. 16.
5. A. H. Almaas, *Inexhaustible Mystery: Diamond Heart Book Five*, Boston: Shambhala, 2011, pp. 261-262.
6. Byron Katie, *I Need Your Love – Is That True?* New York; Random House, 2005.

Chapter 13
1. Samuel Beckett, *Waiting for Godot*, London: Faber and Faber, 1956.
2. Tony Parsons, *As It Is: The Open Secret of Spiritual Awakening*, Carlsbad, CA: Inner Directions Publishing, 2000.

Chapter 14
1. Adyashanti, *Abandon Yourself to Fear*, Pacific Grove, CA: Open Gate Sangha, 2005.(cd)

2. J. Krishnamurti *On Fear*, New York: Harper Collins, 1995, p. 11.
3. Gangaji. *The Diamond in Your Pocket*, Sounds True, Boulder CO, 2005, p. 175.
4. Osho, *The Diamond Sutra*, Pune: Osho International, 1978.
5. J. Krishnamurti, *The First and Last Freedom*, New York: Harper Collins, 1954.

Chapter 15

1. Jed McKenna, *Spiritual Enlightenment: The Damnedest Thing*, USA: Wise FoolPress, 2002, p. 7.
2. For an account, see Gary Nixon and Nancy Sharpe, "Nondual Psychotherapy: Letting Go of the Separate Self Contraction and Embracing Non-Dual Being" *Paradoxica: Journal of Nondual Psychology*, 1 (paradoxica.ca).
3. Katie Davis, *Awake Joy: The Essence of Enlightenment*, Hawaii: Awake Spirit Publishing, 2008, p. 152–154.

Chapter 16

1. A. H. Almaas, *Elements of the Real Man: Diamond Heart Book One*, Boston: Shambhala, 1987, p. 15.
2. Arthur Janov, *The Primal Scream*, New York: Dell, 1970.
3. Fritz Perls, *Gestalt Therapy Verbatim*, Moab, UT: Real People Press, 1969.
    Alexander, Lowen, *Depression and the Body: The Biological Basis of Faith and Reality*, New York: Penguin, 1972.
4. See Marv Westwood & Patricia Wilenksy, *Therapeutic Enactment: Restoring Vitality Through Trauma Repair in Groups*, Vancouver, BC: Group Action Press, 2005.
5. Peter Levine, *Waking the Tiger: Healing Trauma*, Berkeley, CA: North Atlantic Books, 1997.
    Peter Levine, *In an Unspoken Voice: How the Body Releases Trauma and Restores Goodness*, Berkeley, CA: North Atlantic Books, 2010.

Chapter 17

1. Peter Levine, *Waking the Tiger: Healing Trauma,* Berkeley, CA: North Atlantic Books, 1997.
2. Cited in N. Foster & J. Shoemaker, *The Roaring Stream: A New Zen Reader,* Hopewell, NJ: The Ecco Press, 1996, p. 11.
3. Ramesh Balsekar, *Consciousness Speaks,* Los Angeles, CA: Advaita Press, 1992.
4. J. Krishnamurti *On Fear,* New York: Harper Collins, 1995, p. i.
5. Lin Yutang (ed), *The Wisdom of Lao Tse,* New York: Random House, 1948.
6. Osho, *Living Tao (2nd ed.),* Pune, India: Osho International, 2003, p. 6.
7. Osho, *The Art of Dying(2nd ed.),* Pune, India: Osho International, 1999, p.

Chapter 19

1. L. Najavitz, S*eeking Safety: A Treatment Manual for PTSD and Substance Abuse,* New York, NY: The Guilford Press, 2002.
2. P. Ogden, K. Minto, & C. Pain, *Trauma and the Body: A Sensorimotor Approach to Psychotherapy,* New York: W.W.W. Norton, 2006.
3. Peter Levine, *In an Unspoken Voice: How the Body Releases Trauma and Restores Goodness,* Berkeley, CA: North Atlantic Books, 2010, p. 91.
4. Peter Levine, *In an Unspoken Voice: How the Body Releases Trauma and Restores Goodness,* Berkeley, CA: North Atlantic Books, 2010, p. 94.
5. A. H. Almaas, *The Point of Existence: Transformations of Narcissism in Self-Realization,* Boston: Shambhala, 2001, p.337.

Chapter 20

1. Brian Weiss, *Many Lives, Many Masters,* New York: Touchstone, 1988.
2. C. G. Jung, *The Archetypes and the Collective Unconscious, Collected Works of C.G. Jung (2nd ed.),* USA: Princeton University Press, 1980.
3. Stanislav Grof, *The Adventure of Self-Discovery: Dimensions of Consciousness and New Perspectives in Psychotherapy and Inner Exploration,* Albany, NY: State University of New York Press, 1988.

4. Adi Da, *Easy Death (2nd ed.)*, Clearlake, CA: Dawn Horse Press, 1991.

Chapter 21

1. Stanislav Grof, *Beyond the Brain: Birth, Death, and Transcendence in Psychotherapy*, Albany, NY: State University of New York Press, 1985. See also: Stanislav. Grof, *The Adventure of Self-Discovery: Dimensions of Consciousness and New Perspectives in Psychotherapy and Inner Exploration*, Albany, NY: State University of New York Press, 1988. Stanislav Grof, *The Cosmic Game: Explorations of the Frontiers of Human Consciousness*, Albany, NY: State University of New York Press, 1998.
2. Stanislav Grof, *Beyond the Brain: Birth, Death, and Transcendence in Psychotherapy*, Albany, NY: State University of New York Press, 1985, p. 102.
3. p. 106
4. p. 111
5. p. 112
6. p. 116
7. p. 117
8. p. 120
9. p. 122–3
10. p. 123
11. See Grof's website at www.holotropic.com

Chapter 22

1. Adi Da, *Easy Death (2nd ed.)*, Clearlake, CA: Dawn Horse Press, 1991, p. 87.
2. Karl, Renz, *The Myth of Enlightenment*, Carlsbad, CA: Inner Directions, 2005, p. xxi.
3. Chogyam Trungpa *Transcending Madness: The Experience of the Six Bardos*, Boston: Shambhala, 1992.
4. David Hawkins, *Power vs. Force: The Hidden Determinants of Human Behavior*, Carlsbad, CA: Hay House.

5. A. H. Almaas, *The Facets of Unity: The Enneagram of Holy Ideas*, Berkeley, CA: Diamond Books, 1998, p. 50.

Chapter 24

1. Osho, *Autobiography of a Spiritually Incorrect Mystic*, Pune, India: Osho International, 2000.
2. Edward Conze (translator), *Buddhist Wisdom Books*, Allen & Unwin, 1958.
3. Byron Katie, *Loving What Is: Four Questions That Can Change Your Life*, New York: Harmony Books, 2002.
4. Dennis Genpo Merzel, *Big Mind, Big Heart: Finding Your Way*, Salt Lake City: Big Mind Publishing, 2007.
5. See Eleonora Gilbert, *Conversations on Non-duality: Twenty-Six Awakenings*, London: Cherry Red Books, 2011, p. 166.
6. p. 166.
7. pp. 167–168.

Chapter 25

1. See H. W. L. Poonja. *The Truth Is*, York Beach, ME: Samuel Weiser, 2000.
2. See Ken Wilber, *Integral Psychology*, Boston: Shambhala, 2000.

Chapter 26

1. Adyashanti, *Achieving Total Failure*, San Rafael, Ca: Open Gate, 2007, (cd).
2. Edward Conze (translator), *Buddhist Wisdom Books*, G. Allen & Unwin, 1958.
3. Red Pine (translator), *The Zen Teachings of Bodhidharma*, Port Townsend, WA: Empty Bowl, 1987.

Chapter 27

1. Paul Reps, *Zen Flesh, Zen Bones*, Rutland, Vermont: New York: Tuttle, 1957.

2. Lin Yutang (ed.), *The Wisdom of Lao Tse,* New York: Random House, 1948.
3. David Loy, *Lack and Transcendence*, New York: Humanity Books, 1996.

Chapter 28
1. R. H. Blyth, *Zen and Zen Classics*, Tokyo: Hokuseido Press, 1960.
2. Robert Poweell, *The Ultimate Medicine, as Prescribed by Sri Nisargadatta Maharaj*, San Diego, CA: Blue Dove Press, 2001.
3. Karl Renz, *The Myth of Enlightenment,* Carlsbad, CA: Inner Directions, 2005.v
4. H. W. L. Poonja. *The Truth Is*, York Beach, ME: Samuel Weiser, 2000, p. 541.
5. Osho, *The Diamond Sutra,* Pune, India: Osho International, 1979, p. 341.

Chapter 29
1. Lin Yutang (ed.), *The Wisdom of Lao Tse,* New York: Random House, 1948.
2. Lin Yutang (ed.), *The Wisdom of Lao Tse,* New York: Random House, 1948.

CPSIA information can be obtained at www.ICGtesting.com
Printed in the USA
LVOW07s2354160414

382009LV00001B/1/P